1

Introduction: regulation and municipal licensing

PETER QUANCE

The two studies in this volume examine some problems and issues in municipal licensing in Ontario. The questions raised often reflect the broader context of government regulation generally, its intentions, methods, and shortcomings. An understanding of municipal licensing goals and practices thus has to begin with a sense of how they exemplify more general regulatory goals and practices.

Regulation of the private sector is one of several instruments by which governments seek to achieve policy goals. In some cases, for instance, it is seen as an alternative to public ownership. The main purposes of regulation are to compensate for the failure of the market to attain certain ends, to redistribute income, and to achieve certain social and cultural objectives. Regulation can apply to a single industry or to many industries, but in general its approach concentrates on regulating either an activity or the person who undertakes the activity. Licensing is an example of the latter. Regulation can shift benefits between industries and economic sectors, and so is often the focus of much lobbying by interest groups. This fact, along with many others, has led to powerful recent opposition to regulation in general and contributed to current pressures for deregulation in many forms.

Municipal licensing serves a variety of regulatory purposes such as consumer protection and public health and safety. The municipal licensing power is delegated from the provincial government. Up to the present, municipalities have been restricted to a list of enumerated specific powers, and the result has been the growth of a disorganized and unwieldy accumulation of bylaws, many of which are in conflict or obsolete. The development of a two-tier system of municipal government, as exemplified by Metropolitan Toronto, adds to the complexity of the issues. However, it seems possible to envisage a reorganized system in which provincial and municipal powers will be exercised more rationally to deal with problems at the level they tend to occur.

REGULATION: AN OVERVIEW

Regulation may be defined in many ways, reflecting its wide-ranging impact in many sectors of the economy. Perhaps it is best defined as 'a state-imposed limitation on the discretion that may be exercised by individuals or organizations which is supported by the threat of sanction.'[1] As a result, regulation is most pertinent when decision-making is apportioned between the private and public segments of the economy. Though government regulation of economic behaviour has become increasingly pervasive and complex in the last couple of decades, it is as old as government itself. For instance, *The Wealth of Nations* by Adam Smith was prompted by the regulatory control of the state under mercantilism.[2] The regulatory thrust has spread into many new areas, as evidenced by the spate of rules which emerged in the late 1960s to protect the environment. Regulatory intervention by government in the private sector is not, therefore, a recent phenomenon, though concern over the degree of intervention may be rising.

Regulation as a policy instrument

Governments can employ several instruments to influence economic behaviour. These include exhortation, negotiation, and moral suasion such as threats of action or the creation of government bodies. Direct expenditures, such as grants, subsidies, or transfer payments, can be used to induce the recipients to alter their intended course of action. Another alternative with much the same effect is tax expenditures, such as exemptions, where the cost is measured in revenue forgone instead of monies expended directly.

Direct or indirect taxation, fees, or prices for public services are other powerful instruments at the disposition of governments. Public ownership, including joint ventures, can also be employed.

Regulation is frequently an effective government tool. Like the other instruments, it can be applied flexibly. For instance, it can be used to prohibit an activity where the risk is so high the marginal damage exceeds the marginal benefit. Activities can also be separated through regulatory activities such as zoning. Regulatory standards – for example, minimum or exact criteria – are useful in achieving public policy goals. Unlike some of the other policy instruments though, regulation is not voluntary. In this sense it differs from both tax and direct expenditures where the recipient can choose not to accept the inducement.

The merits of each policy instrument should also be weighed. For instance, regulation must be judged against the economic and social performance of the unregulated market. Even if a regulated market leads to an improvement in

1 Stone, *Regulation and its Alternatives*, Congressional Quarterly Press, Washington DC, 1982, 10
2 This example was cited in *Responsible Regulation*, an Interim Report by the Economic Council of Canada, November 1979, Ottawa, 10.

social terms, it may not be the most desirable approach if the economic costs of the regulatory policies outweigh the benefits. The political costs and benefits will also be important to the policy decision-makers. The best instrument for the problem in question must also be chosen.

Frequently, the political costs of using regulation to achieve policy goals appear to be lower than many of the alternatives: taxation, direct expenditures, or public ownership.[3] The budgetary costs of administering even a pervasive regulatory program are relatively small. Greater costs are usually borne in the private sector by consumers and workers. The latter costs are often more subtle because they will frequently be hidden in the prices of goods or services.

Objectives of regulation
Aside from the previously discussed political and bureaucratic reasons for regulation, there can be justification for government intervention in certain circumstances. The primary purposes for government regulation are to compensate for market failure, to redistribute income, or to achieve social and cultural objectives.

1 Compensation for market failure
Market failure has been defined as a 'situation where the excess of benefits over costs under the free market's use of resources is less than under an alternative arrangement, such as regulation.'[4] Both direct and social regulation have been used to address market failures.

The classic example of market failure occurs in the case of a *natural monopoly*, when costs are lowest with only one producer. Production is characterized by declining average and marginal cost curves. This implies high fixed initial costs, as with utilities, often cited as the best example of natural monopolies. Characteristic of natural monopolies are firms that supply continuous or repeated services through permanent physical connections between the supplier's plant and the consumers. In a natural monopoly the bargaining power of consumers is also often weak. Given the size of the firms involved, this type of regulation is largely outside the municipal sphere. However, Palmer suggests in his contribution to this volume that some smaller cities may only be able to support one or two taxi firms profitably, especially if the dispatch business is important, so that an argument can be made for fare regulation in some cases.

Destructive competition is another form of market failure often cited as a reason for regulatory intervention. According to this view, in the absence of regulation the industry, or at least parts of it, will operate at a loss for long periods of time. This could result in a deterioration of service and in some cases safety levels. Therefore,

3 Ibid., 43
4 See Stone, *Regulation*, 63.

entry controls are necessary. The chief prerequisites for destructive competition are substantial excess capacity and rigidities that retard the reallocation of capital and labour. For a firm to operate for a long period of time at a loss, a high proportion of costs must be fixed so that the firm may be willing to just cover variable cost and avoid closing down and losing the substantial investment in fixed assets.

Destructive competition is often cited by the taxi industry to justify regulation. However, the rigidities do not appear to be present in that industry, which, with its unskilled labour and low capital costs, should feature relatively easy entry and exit in the absence of government intervention.

Externalities can also justify government intervention. These occur where there is a divergence between private and social costs and private and social benefits. The classic example of an externality occurs environmentally where one party will rationalize its actions according to its private costs while ignoring the social costs borne by surrounding parties. Costs are not all internalized in private market transactions for three basic reasons: the absence of property rights in some valuable resources, high transaction costs, and imperfect information.[5]

At the local level, land use regulation controls externalities through the use of zoning bylaws. As discussed by Bossons and Makuch below, this mechanism limits municipalities to control over land by standards set out in advance, which greatly hampers their flexibility. Their control could be more effective and more responsive if they were able to operate on a case-by-case basis. Bossons and Makuch suggest that municipalities be allowed to license land, a power that could be used along with the present zoning powers to create a more comprehensive system. For instance, externalities in the form of noise could be curtailed more easily if the user's licence is subject to revocation than under the zoning system which regulates the use of land.

Market failure can also occur because of *information disparities*. These can prevent individuals from making the fully informed decisions that would have been made if more information had been provided on, for instance, a particular service that is offered in the market. As pointed out by Bossons and Makuch, adequate information will not be produced privately where the private seller can make little use of a 'brand name.' This often occurs in a market dominated by small firms which make few repeat sales. Municipal regulation often deals with firms and individuals in just such a market.

Where adequate information is not available, the government must still decide how far it should intervene in an attempt to remedy the situation and, if regulation is appropriate, determine the most effective form. Even where intervention would lead to improved decision-making on the part of individuals, the costs to the

5 See *Responsible Regulation*, 48.

government in providing the information since it is not a costless good, and the costs to producers – of increased educational requirements for instance – which may be passed along in the form of higher prices to individuals, must be compared to the benefits provided by improved information. In some instances, these benefits could be quite small if competitive pressures force firms to provide a fair amount of information. Bossons and Makuch suggest that in some markets, such as those for skilled tradesmen, the benefits may outweigh the costs.

2 Redistribution of income

Redistribution of income to certain groups is sometimes stated to be an objective of regulation. An example occurs in the case of taxicabs where it has been argued that without regulation no one could earn an adequate income. Proponents of this approach make arguments analogous to those advanced in support of minimum wage legislation. However, regulation does not directly address the question of wages, so that its main impact is usually a lower demand for the services of cab drivers. Regulation can also attempt to redistribute resources to groups of consumers. One example noted by Palmer would be fare discounts to senior citizens.

3 Social goals

Different levels of government have resorted to regulation in an attempt to achieve social and cultural goals. This is frequently evident at the federal level where the government attempts to encourage Canadian content in radio and television. Municipal governments often try to legislate public morality by means of licensing. For instance, in Metropolitan Toronto licences are required to operate 'adult entertainment parlours' and 'body rub parlours,' a requirement that enables the municipality to regulate both extensively.

The scope of regulation

Some regulation is industry-specific. For example, prices in the form of fares or rates can be controlled. A prime example of this is found in the taxicab industry as discussed in Palmer. In fact, only one reasonably sized Canadian city, Fredericton, has not established a fare structure for taxicabs. Over half of them also restrict entry by potential operators.[6]

Supply of a product can also be regulated by governments through licences, franchises, permits, and quotas. This is done by restricting entry or in some cases exit, as is done by licensing in the taxi industry. Licensing is one of the prime regulatory tools for local governments. Control over rates of return and output are

6 See Papillon, 'The taxi industry and its regulation in Canada,' Working Paper No. 30, Ottawa, Economic Council of Canada, March 1982, 9–13.

other illustrations of direct regulation. Examples of the former include pipelines and telephones, while marketing boards typify the latter.

Other regulation, such as 'equity' regulation, which includes protection against fraud or inaccurate information, applies more widely. As pointed out by Bossons and Makuch, a great deal of municipal licensing falls into this category. Similar regulation has developed concerning health and safety, environmental issues, and land use controls. 'Cultural' regulation in a municipal setting includes bylaws aimed at controlling morality, such as those mentioned above requiring the licensing of body rub parlours and adult entertainment parlours.

Regulation that attempts to control the attributes of goods or services or monitor information disclosure is very common in municipal licensing. Efforts to improve information available to consumers or ensure minimum standards in the provision of services undoubtedly reflect the belief that information will be costly to obtain for many consumers.

Methods of production are also modified by social regulation. Environmental or health and safety standards, along with many occupational licensing criteria, attempt to protect parties from making decisions that they will later regret. Conditions of sale or employment can also be subject to regulation which dictates provisions affecting store hours or anti-discrimination requirements.

Two basic approaches to regulation
Two basic types of regulatory approaches can be employed. Regulation can concentrate either on the activity or on the person who provides a good or service. The former, less restrictive, approach can be used when it is relatively inexpensive for individuals to evaluate the available information. It is more appropriate if there is a lesser degree of skill involved in the profession or trade of the producer, where standards are quite easy to impose, and where the risk of harm to the consumer is quite slight.

Basically, there are three techniques for regulating an activity: information regulation, performance standards, and specification standards.[7] Information regulation requires a certain minimum amount of information to be provided. It is often used where the degree of risk is minimal. Information disclosure minimizes government involvement but is inadequate where complex information must be conveyed to allow consumers to make an informed choice. Regulating the allowable fares and posting the fee structure on the exterior of taxicabs is an example discussed by Palmer.

Performance standards establish a minimum result that must be obtained, leaving the producer free to determine the least costly way to comply. The

7 Stone, *Regulation*, 161

producing firm is more closely regulated under specification standards in that both the standard and the method of achieving that standard is the subject of government decree. For instance, standards of mechanical fitness, compulsory equipment, and a minimum number of doors could be prescribed for taxis.

If regulation aims instead at the person practising the trade or occupation, the government again has the choice of four regulatory techniques at its disposal: licensing, certification, registration, and permits.

Under the first, a licence is required before the trade or occupation can be practised. Licensing has been defined as 'the ability to prohibit an individual from engaging in a lawful activity without government approval' and its purpose characterized as 'to regulate activities of a legal nature for the public good of the community.'[8] Licensing also can be a useful tool in a regulatory scheme where a licence is issued on condition that the licensee comply with regulations established by the government. Often, obtaining a licence is dependent on the fulfillment of certain education requirements or the meeting of other standards such as being of good character. While this can help ensure that skilled people are providing services, in practice it frequently also has the undesirable side effect of reducing the supply of that service. It is axiomatic then that prices will rise. In the case of taxicabs, the numbers are often explicitly limited without any reference to qualifying requirements.

Regulation over the person can also be achieved by certification. Under this system, anyone could practise a skill or profession, but only those who have fulfilled certain requirements, based for example on training or education, could use a particular designation. This would still provide some information to consumers while avoiding the adverse side effects of reduced supply and higher prices.

Registration is little more than a list of individuals or firms who participate in a certain activity. It conveys no information about a producer's qualifications but can help prevent or detect theft or fraud by making identification easier. For taxicabs it could very well be a more appropriate device than licensing.[9] Since many of the tests for other trades currently licensed by municipalities focus on good character, registration might be more appropriate in those instances also. If licensing is not actually enforced, it in effect becomes a registry.

Permits can also be employed. They are useful for granting permission for a single act of short duration, unlike a licence, which generally allows someone to engage in an activity over an extended period of time.

While these regulatory measures may sound effective, in practice they can fall

8 See Municipality of Metropolitan Toronto, Chief Administrative Officers Department, 'Review of the Licensing Function in Metropolitan Toronto,' November, 1977, 18.

9 Stone, *Regulation*, 157

short. Specification of quality can be very difficult.[10] If a tradesman passes an examination to obtain a licence, that is no guarantee of the future quality of his practice. In these and other cases, such as serious car defects, liability assigned through litigation or by guarantees may prove more effective than regulation.

Support for regulation

The impetus towards collective decision-making through regulation, as opposed to reliance on an unfettered market, receives a major boost through the self-interest of many large segments in the economy.[11] Most regulation is the product of a variety of such forces operating in society, and the extent to which it coincides with the goals of many interest groups must be understood.

The ability of governments to reduce competition through devices such as tariffs, marketing boards, and licensing also provides a powerful incentive for groups to organize and channel that power to their advantage.[12]

Often some producers will seek an advantage for themselves by promoting regulation of their industry, perhaps in the form of barriers to entry or occupational licensing. The ability of taxi drivers to limit their own numbers is decried in Palmer's study.[13] Regulation can also retard the operation of market forces. To the extent that groups cannot adapt quickly to changing technologies, the regulatory process frequently offers some protection.[14]

While consumers frequently are the victims of higher prices due to the barriers erected at the behest of the producers, one group of consumers can often benefit at the expense of another. For example, through utility rate regulation one group of consumers could secure cross-subsidization of their requirements by other consumers. Similarly, users of non-economic airline routes can be subsidized by riders on more heavily travelled routes.

Once regulation is instituted, the self-interest of beneficiaries who operate the regulatory apparatus acts as a powerful incentive in favour of the status quo or even

10 See Price, *Sunset Legislation in the United States*, State Bar of Texas, Austin, September 1977, 16.
11 Trebilcock, Waverman, and Prichard, 'Markets for regulation: implications for performance standards and institutional design,' in *Government Regulation: Issues and Alternatives*, 1978, Ontario Economic Council, Toronto, 30–74, discuss the interests of various groups who may be aided by regulation.
12 Breton, *The Regulation of Private Economic Activity*, C.D. Howe Research Institute, Montreal, 1976, 11
13 See Papillon, 'The taxi industry,' 30.
14 Owen and Braeutigan, *The Regulation Game: Strategic Use of the Administrative Process*, Cambridge, Mass., Ballinger Publishing Company, 1978, 18–23
15 Tulloch, 'The transactional gains trap,' *Bell Journal of Economics*, vol. 6, no. 2 (Autumn 1975), discusses this concept as it applies to taxicab licences, 672.

more regulation. Bureaucrats will see a continuation of regulation as employment insurance and a means of advancing in the governmental hierarchy. The natural inclination of regulatory agencies is to expand their horizons and increase their amount of regulation, so that they will be perceived as vigorously fulfilling their function and will be meeting the most common and discernible yardstick for measuring their performance. 'Secondary industries' such as lawyers and accountants are often employed on the basis of their expertise in a particular regulatory area. Naturally, their self-interest will dictate support for continued or expanded regulation.

Frequently, groups being regulated will also have a powerful economic stake in the continuation of regulation. Windfall gains occurring from barriers to entry, for example, tend to be quickly capitalized so that subsequent investments tend to realize relatively normal rates of return. If that industry is deregulated, huge capital losses would quickly occur. Nowhere is this more apparent than in the case of taxicabs, where the high price of licences in cities such as Toronto gives licence holders a significant stake in continuing the present system. For this reason Palmer recommends that the removal of entry restrictions in the taxi industry be achieved gradually.

Politicians, the ultimate arbiters of the acceptable level of regulatory activity, often will be vulnerable to the pressures of the various interest groups in favour of expanded regulation. Though the welfare of a majority of the populace may be ameliorated by less regulation, these advantages will often be difficult to perceive. Thus, a small group with a large stake in regulation will often be able to mount more effective political pressure than the less interested majority. This pressure will frequently reinforce an already existing bias in favour of intervention. To the extent that inperfections exist in the markets, as is often the case, politicians will be inclined to intervene. Doing nothing about a problem is usually not politically feasible, and, as was mentioned earlier, the political costs attached to regulation are often less than is the case with an alternative instrument. Therefore, regulation proliferates.

The push for deregulation
In the preceding pages the discussion has centred on the reasons regulation has come to occupy such a prominent role in the economy. Powerful forces such as interest groups have been able to wield enough influence to achieve regulation that is not necessarily in the larger public good. Frequently, the political process is skewed towards intervention, which often means more regulation. In many cases, this move to regulation can be supported by economic justifications such as a need to correct market failure.

Despite the powerful forces in favour of regulation in the last decade, there has been a reaction in favour of less regulation. Part of this new attitude may have originated in concern over the slowing of economic growth and the reduction in Canada's international competitiveness, which have helped contribute to higher levels of unemployment and inflation.[16] Regulation has been blamed for shifting scarce resources away from uses that could improve productivity and foster innovation. Even in cases of market failure where some regulation is warranted, there has been the feeling that the amount of regulation has not been justified by the problem. Complementing this approach, a more stringent evaluation of the cost effectiveness of various regulatory schemes could assist in moulding regulation into a more effective instrument.

Paralleling concerns over the economic performance of regulation has been a political backlash. Many citizens share the belief that the regulatory process is unresponsive to public opinion and the wishes of elected representatives. In their view, regulatory agencies have become unresponsive to shifting public needs and have outgrown their original purposes.[17] The view that regulatory bodies have been enjoying unfettered growth, often only to serve the groups that are supposed to be regulated, has gained credence with the proliferation of government agencies. Business complaints about the rapid growth of government regulation and expenditures became more insistent in the 1960s and 1970s. In Canada, this concern was reinforced by the imposition of wage and price controls in 1975. Sluggish economic performance and a heightened political scepticism of regulation have contributed to the recent interest in regulatory reform and deregulation.

Deregulatory measures
Significant steps towards regulatory reform can be made in several ways. More extensive use of cost benefit techniques can be employed, such as compelling regulatory bodies to be guided by two budgets.[18] One would involve the usual appropriations while the other would assign an upper allowable limit to costs resulting from the agency's actions. Once that limit is reached, old regulations would have to be repealed before new ones could be instituted. This approach would entail some practical problems in determining costs. Other possible reform measures include building greater public participation into the proceedings of regulatory bodies and restricting employment in the regulatory agencies. Among other regulatory reform possibilities are advance notice of regulatory changes in policy to encourage public participation and minimize any adverse impact.

16 Stone, *Regulation*, 240
17 Price, *Sunset Legislation*, 11
18 Stone, *Regulation*, 14

1 Sunset legislation

Sunset legislation is another means of instituting regulatory reform. Because it has been a hotly debated technique and because it was included in the draft Municipal Licensing Act and considered below by Bossons and Makuch, sunset legislation will be discussed more fully here than some other reform proposals.

The concept of sunset legislation, which first became prominent in the mid-1970s, is designed to improve the legislative control over regulatory bodies. Sunset legislation generally establishes a timetable for review of programs, laws, and agencies. After a certain length of time an automatic termination of the subject of the review would occur unless it is considered valuable enough to be continued. Obviously, a thorough preliminary study is needed so that an informed decision on termination can be made. As a result, the customary onus in favour of continuation is reversed so that termination will occur unless the program has merit. According to proponents of sunset legislation, the performance of regulatory bodies should be improved, and obsolete or inefficient programs will be eliminated. Therefore, the essential features of a sunset program are (1) regular and periodic review, (2) automatic termination, and (3) a system to assess performance.

The scope of sunset reviews can be varied. A comprehensive review would scrutinize virtually every government entity. This has the advantage of maintaining equity and therefore credibility in the review process. However, it would greatly increase the legislative workload, require increased staff, and almost certainly lead to a more cursory evaluation process. A proper examination would be a detailed time-consuming process. With little in-depth evaluation, there is not likely to be much change from the present, rendering the review process largely impotent.[19] In addition, since it is a new process, full-scale implementation might immediately discredit the program if it does not function smoothly right from the start.

Another approach is to single out a few selected trouble spots for evaluation and possible termination. This may create problems with those who feel that singling out a few programs is inequitable. However, it may meet the criticisms of those who feel that most sunset approaches are too institutionalized and waste resources by mandatory, unnecessary, or untimely reviews. Many argue that predetermined reviews are inappropriate because the natural life of programs' cycle differ.[20] Conversely, those in favour of fixed review periods allege that they are needed to institutionalize and reinforce the sunset process.[21]

---

19 See Sloan and Flynn, 'Sunset: it's not all rosy,' *Sunset in Perspective: A Critical Analysis*, New York State Assembly, February 1978, 88–115, at 95.
20 See Friedman, 'Introduction,' ibid., 7.
21 See Adams and Sherman (1978), 'Sunset implementation: a positive partnership to make government work,' 38 *Public Administration Review*, 78–81, at 78.

A third approach is to apply the sunset process to all bodies that perform regulatory or licensing functions. Actual sunset experience so far indicates that the legislation can be more useful in reviewing regulatory bodies.[22] By focusing on a small portion of the government's apparatus, the dangers of overloading the system and producing superficial evaluations are minimized. Some degree of equity is also retained. While regulatory bodies do not usually have large budgets, they can have a significant cost impact on the economy. Frequently, they are not well scrutinized during the budget process.[23] For these reasons the sunset approach appears to be more appropriate for implementing regulatory reform than if used on a wholesale basis throughout government.

In adopting a sunset system generally for its advertising agencies, Ontario appears to have followed a prudent, selective approach. Currently, advisory agencies face sunset deadlines after an Agency Review Committee was appointed in March 1978.

2 Deregulation in municipal licensing

The draft Municipal Licensing Act, not enacted five years after it was first announced, stated that a bylaw is deemed to be repealed after a period of five years.[24] Therefore, all municipal licensing bylaws will be subject to sunset review. Based on the principles adumbrated above, they appear to be good candidates for such a review. They are a selected portion of overall government activity, are part of the regulatory process, and are often outdated or in need of review.

The various draft municipal licensing bills have attempted to encourage deregulation in another way as well. As originally envisioned by the provincial government, there would have been no provisions allowing municipalities to collect fees from the businesses being licensed. The government argued that since the purpose of licensing is to protect the public from unfair business practices, the costs should be borne out of general revenues. It was also felt that the no-fee provision would encourage municipalities to deregulate and license only when it was in the interests of the general public to do so.[25]

Municipalities, however, objected strenuously to the no-fee provisions in the draft legislation. They felt that the licences would not be taken seriously without a fee. In addition, they argued that since some of the benefit accrues to the licence holder, he should bear some of the administrative costs of the licensing program.

22 See Friedman, 'Introduction,' 5.
23 See Adams and Sherman, 'Sunset implementation,' 80.
24 See S. 6 of Bill 11 of the 2nd session of the 32nd Legislature, Ontario. This is the latest in a series of bills which have appeared but have not been passed since municipal licensing reform was first announced by Darcy McKeough, minister of treasury, economics and intergovernmental affairs, on 15 April 1977.
25 See the Ontario Legislative Debates, 1 June 1978, 3016.

Finally, municipalities stated that out-of-town customers who utilized municipal services would escape paying any portion of the costs but would still enjoy the protection provided by the licence.

As a result of this pressure, the 1982 draft Municipal Licensing Act, Bill 11, allowed fees to be set by the municipalities to recover administrative and enforcement costs or, alternatively, prescribes set levels of $10 or $25, the higher amount being allowed if an inspection is required. Exceptions to this regime are allowed for 'body rub parlours,' 'adult entertainment parlours', and taxicabs, where higher fees can be charged.

The lobbying by municipalities against the disallowance of fees illustrates the difficulties often encountered in implementing a deregulatory proposal. It also emphasizes the subservient position of municipalities, which forces them to plead their case before a higher level of government because they do not possess unequivocal powers themselves.

MUNICIPAL LICENSING

Purposes of municipal licensing

Municipal licensing for the purpose of raising revenue and for the purpose of regulation could be considered two separate powers. However, from a legal and conceptual standpoint, at least in Ontario, any distinction appears to be academic. Though the powers may be exercised separately, they have effectively been merged into one omnibus licensing authority subject to the same legal principles. This result will in turn flow through to municipalities when the province delegates some or all of its licensing authority.

In practical terms it appears that the revenue-raising function does not play an important part in municipal licensing. The provincial government has indicated that the municipal power to license should be used to protect the public and not to raise revenue for the municipality.[26] The province's moves to limit licensing fees to a cost-recovery basis reinforce this view. Most municipalities have argued for cost-recovery fees and share the province's view that the licensing of business should be for purely regulatory purposes and should not be a general source of revenue.[27] As an illustration of this, municipal revenues in 1978 from licences and permits totalled only 0.39 per cent of total municipal revenues.[28]

26 Statement on Municipal Licensing by Darcy McKeough, minister of treasury, economics and intergovernmental affairs, 15 April 1977.
27 The Association of Municipalities of Ontario, *Submission to the Standing Committee of the Ontario Legislature on the Administration of Justice regarding Bill 11 – an Act to Provide for the Licensing of Businesses by Municipalities*, 22 July 1982, 7.
28 Ibid., Table II.

Municipal licensing bylaws can, and do, cover a host of areas and fulfil many varying purposes, besides dealing with contentious issues like body rub parlours and adult entertainment parlours. Many of the different areas, barbers for example, are discussed by Bossons and Makuch. In licensing the various trades and services many purposes are met, such as enforcing minimum standards of competence, protecting the public health, keeping a record of people holding the licence, and ensuring public safety.

Consumer protection is another function which may be fulfilled through the licensing function. A regulatory bylaw can deal with improper conduct by tradesmen. This regime can be greatly strengthened when coupled with a licensing bylaw. For instance, a tradesman may find it more difficult to sue for the price of work done if he is unlicensed.[29] A licensing inspector can also assist in a civil lawsuit against a tradesman by testifying or giving some idea of the expected outcome. Also, as Bossons and Makuch mention, municipal licensing can be a useful adjunct to provincial legislation in the consumer protection field. The threat of having a licence revoked can also make regulation more effective where rates must be posted in taxicabs or in the regulation of business hours or when requiring that adequate insurance be obtained. Some of these regulations are recognizable as attempts to deal with market failures which are, as discussed earlier, an important economic justification for regulation.

Sources of municipal licensing power
There are three major levels of government in Canada: municipal, provincial, and federal. However, only the latter two have constitutional status. Since municipalities do not have their own constitutional source of power, they must depend on delegated authority from the higher levels of government, almost exclusively the provincial. This position is tenuous because municipal authority can be removed by the mere amendment of a statute.

Provinces can rely on several constitutional heads of authority when overseeing the municipal licensing function. S. 92(9) of the BNA Act empowers provincial legislatures to make laws relating to 'Shop, Saloon, Tavern, Auctioneer, and other Licences in order to the raising of a Revenue for Provincial, Local or Municipal Purposes.' This allows a province to raise revenues through licensing and, within that sphere, delegate the power to municipalities.

Other heads of provincial power under the BNA Act also bolster the licensing function. Through S. 92(8) the provinces have authority over 'municipal institutions.' S. 92(13) gives the provinces power over 'property and civil rights,' while S. 92(16) governs 'matters of a merely local or private nature.' The regulatory

---

29 See Rust-D'Eye, 'Municipal licensing: enabling legislation and bylaws' (1981); 2 *Advocates Quarterly*, at 439.

powers which flow from these sections can be exercised by means of licences. It is now clear that a provincial legislature has the authority to levy licence fees in support of a regulatory scheme because they are regarded as charges for services rather than taxes.[30]

Restrictive delegation

Before municipalities can enact licensing bylaws, the authority to do so must be delegated from the provincial government. Ontario licensing provisions in the Municipal Act delegate the power to 'license, regulate, and govern' a long list of enumerated powers. Without the grant of a specific power, municipalities cannot act. In tying municipalities to specific provisions in the Municipal Act, an awkward and cumbersome system has evolved which severely limits the ability of municipalities to react to new concerns. This has reinforced the subservient role of municipalities with respect to the province. The draft Municipal Licensing Act attempted to remedy this problem by giving municipalities a general power to license, regulate, and govern without requiring specific authorization for each trade or occupation. If a new municipal problem crops up, the need for the legislatures to decide whether it is occurring on a province-wide basis, and if so to amend the legislation, will be eliminated. However, taxis are kept separate from the general power, a move which, among other things, allows restrictions on entry to be maintained. Municipalities have been given this general power in British Columbia, Alberta, and Saskatchewan and have not responded with excessive regulatory zeal.[31]

As the recipients of delegated powers, municipalities are not able to act in an unbridled manner through licensing bylaws. The courts have sometimes applied a liberal construction to bylaws which appeared to be *prima facie* within the scope and intent of the enabling legislation.[32] This was done on the premise that municipal elected representatives are well situated to respond to local concerns. However, the courts apply several rules of strict construction to municipal bylaws which interfere with the common law rights of citizens, particularly the right to carry on a lawful business. For instance, municipalities have not been able to refuse licences on grounds that are extraneous to the purpose of the enabling legislation, which up to now has been the Municipal Act in Ontario. This approach has helped prevent municipalities from refusing a licence for zoning reasons

30 La Forest, *The Allocation of Taxing Power under the Canadian Constitution*, 2nd edition, Canadian Tax Foundation, Toronto, May 1981, 161
31 See *Review of the Licensing Function*, 20.
32 See Rust-D'Eye, 'Municipal licensing,' 441. Among the cases cited in support of this point are *City of Montreal* v. *Morgan* (1920), 60 s.c.r. 393, 54 d.l.r. 165, (1920); 3 w.w.r. 36 and *Kruse* v. *Johnson* (1898) 2 q.b. 91 (Div. Ct.)

because municipalities draw the powers to control the use of land from other legislation – the Planning Act in Ontario.[33] It is this curtailment of municipal flexibility in the use of the licensing function that attracts a great deal of criticism from Bossons and Makuch.

Traditionally, in overseeing the powers delegated to municipalities, the courts have insisted that municipal legislation be subject to provincial legislation. Therefore, any municipal bylaw that conflicts with the provisions of a provincial statute or encroaches into an area occupied by provincial legislation will be struck down. This approach was explicitly contained in the draft Municipal Licensing Act.[34] Where no inconsistency or conflict exists between the provincial and municipal legislation, they can coexist.[35] In that case, municipal bylaws can be utilized to supplement provincial legislation in, for example, the consumer protection or health and safety fields. For instance, enforcement could be easier if done at the municipal level. As emphasized by Bossons and Makuch, this can be one of the most valuable functions of municipal licensing.

Municipalities are also restricted because they have no greater powers than their delegating authority, the province. Any licensing bylaw that is constitutionally *ultra vires* the province will also be beyond the powers of the municipality. For instance, if the licensing bylaw is in pith and substance an exercise of criminal law power, it would be in the exclusive jurisdiction of the federal government and *ultra vires* the municipal government.

In recent years municipalities have striven through licensing bylaws to control establishments that offend community morality standards. Metropolitan Toronto has enacted bylaws designed to license, regulate, and govern 'adult entertainment parlours', which are premises where services are provided that 'appeal to or are designed to appeal to erotic or sexual appetites or inclinations.' Another portion of Metropolitan Toronto's licensing bylaw deals with 'body rub parlours.' A 'body rub' includes the 'kneading, manipulating, touching, or stimulating of a person's body' but does not include medical or therapeutic treatment performed by someone qualified to do so under Ontario law.[36] These bylaws take their authority from provisions in the Municipal Act which were inserted in the draft Municipal

---

33 See Rust-D'Eye, 'Morality and municipal licensing: the untouched constitutional issues in *City of Prince George* v. *Payne*' (1978), 16 *Osgoode Hall Law Journal*, 767–8.

34 *Re Morrison and City of Kingston* (1938) o.r. 21, (1937) 4 d.l.r. 740, 69 c.c.c. 251 (o.c.a.) and *Re Aston and Metropolitan Licensing Commission* (1966) 1 o.r 51, 52 d.l.r. 2 403 (h.c.t.) S.2(7) of Bill 11 confirms that where a licensing bylaw conflicts with a provincial statute or regulation, the latter will prevail.

35 See, for instance, *R. ex rel Dixon* v. *Knapman* (1953) o.w.n. 541, 106 c.c.c. 59 (q.c.a.) and other cases noted by Rust-D'Eye, 'Municipal licensing,' 431.

36 Municipality of Metropolitan Toronto Bylaw 107–78 as amended, S-1

Licensing Act separate from the general licensing provision in that Act. This allows expanded powers in the area. In addition, body rub and adult entertainment parlours, along with taxicabs, are exempted from the customary cost-recovery basis for fees. For instance, adult entertainment parlour fees are now $1650 for a six-month period.[37]

Metropolitan Toronto's adult entertainment parlour licensing bylaw has been attacked on the basis that, among other things, it deals with criminal law, not property and civil rights, and so is beyond municipal competence. It has been held that the bylaw and enabling legislation are regulatory in nature as they are aimed at licensing, regulating, governing, classifying, and inspecting businesses and do not deal with morality, indecency, or obscenity – Criminal Code offences – directly. This allows Metropolitan Toronto to lay down standards of conduct for the protection of its citizens[38] and follows similar decisions in Winnipeg, Vancouver, and Edmonton.[39] By being allowed to license in this area of social values, an important regulatory tool has been preserved for municipalities which decide to impose rules on these types of establishment according to their community standards.

Rationale for delegating to municipalities
From before the time of Confederation, provinces have delegated to municipalities regulatory and licensing powers over businesses. Therefore, the usefulness of municipal government in this area was established at an early date. In introducing the draft Municipal Licensing Act, the Province of Ontario had gone on record as stating that one of the principles behind the new legislation was to strengthen the ability of municipal councils to make licensing decisions.[40]

At the municipal level it is often easier to match the amount and type of regulation with differing local needs. Government responsiveness to consumer concerns can also be improved in some instances if done at the local level. As mentioned before, inadequate information can lead to market failure. Often information about the competence of tradesmen, for example, can be circulated much more easily at the municipal level. Bossons and Makuch also argue persuasively that many negative externalities associated with land uses should be

---

37 Bylaw 107-78 as amended by bylaw 125-82
38 *Sharlmak Hotels Limited* v. *Municipality of Metropolitan Toronto* (1981) 14 M.P.L.R. 260, 32 O.R. 2nd 129, 121 D.L.R. (3rd) 415 (Div. Ct.).
39 See respectively, *Cal Invt. Ltd.* v. *City of Winnipeg* (1978) 84 D.L.R. (3rd) 699. 6 M.P.L.R. 31 (Man C.A.); *Re Vancouver License By-Law 4957* (1978) 5 B.C.L.R. 193, 6 M.P.L.R. 39, 83 D.L.R. (3rd) 236 and *Moffat* v. *City of Edmonton* (1978) 5 Alta. L.R. 2nd 174, 12 A.R. 418. 84 D.L.R. (3rd) 699 affirmed 9 Alta. L.R. 2nd 79, 15 A.R. 530, 99 D.L.R. (3rd) 101 (C.A.).
40 Statement by Darcy McKeough on municipal licensing, 15 April 1977

regulated through licensing at the local level where officials are most likely to be responsive to local variations in regulatory needs.

Counterbalancing the increased flexibility of regulating and licensing at the local level are some disadvantages inherent in delegating to municipalities. There is always the worry about the abuse of discretionary powers by municipal politicians. In addition, differing regulatory standards across the province will impose heavier costs on regulated parties who operate in more than one municipal jurisdiction because they will be forced to adapt to several licensing schemes.

There can be no doubt that the various local governments in Ontario have both varying abilities to license and differing perceptions of the need to license. For instance, Hamilton uses forty licensing provisions, while Port Elgin employs eight.[41] Generally, larger municipalities license more extensively, no doubt reflecting their greater resources. Information-providing mechanisms are also likely to be more useful in the more impersonal, larger centres. This reinforces the need for greater municipal autonomy in meeting different needs, although in some smaller centres there could be a possibility of inadequate licensing to protect consumers if the municipality lacks resources.

The upper tier: Metropolitan Toronto
In most areas of the province, licensing is done by local governments such as villages, towns, cities, and townships. Many of the largest urban areas of the province now have regional governments and are thus two-tier municipalities. In Toronto, all licensing functions are performed by the Metropolitan Toronto government, the upper-tier municipality. Some licensing is also done by other regional governments in the province, including Niagara, Sudbury, York, and Waterloo.[42] However, no other regional government possesses licensing powers comparable in scope to those of Metropolitan Toronto.

At the time of the formation of the regional government in Toronto in 1953, licensing was left with the area municipalities. In 1956, after the unification of Metro's police forces, the Metropolitan Licensing Commission was formed – a significant step in the trend towards licensing on a regional basis. After 1956, the Metropolitan Licensing Commission performed both adjudicative and legislative functions for the fifty-six trades and occupations it licensed shortly after its formation. In 1969, Metropolitan Council assumed the legislative role, and the Metropolitan Licensing Commission became responsible for implementing policies established by the Metropolitan Council.[43]

41 Association of Municipalities of Ontario, *Submission*, Table 1
42 Ontario, Ministry of Treasury, Economics and Intergovernmental Affairs, *Municipal Licensing Discussion Paper*, April 1976, 11
43 Ontario, *Report of the Royal Commission on Metropolitan Toronto* (Robarts Report), Toronto, Queen's Printer, 1977, 288

This meshed well with the contemporary recommendations of the McRuer Report, which urged that licensing legislation should be effected by elected representatives at the local level.[44] However, in many cities of the province some licensing functions are the responsibility of the Police Commission. The Draft Municipal Licensing Act would have transferred to city councils the power to pass licensing bylaws, a continuation of the trend that started with Metropolitan Toronto to give elected councils more licensing power. The Metropolitan Licensing Commission is a tribunal with quasi-judicial duties. Its principal power is to exercise its discretion to grant, refuse, suspend, or revoke licences. The Licensing Commission consists of the chairman of Metropolitan Council or his delegate and two persons appointed by Metropolitan Council who are not members of an area municipality.

S. 10 of Metropolitan Toronto's licensing bylaw states that the Commission, in considering licence applications, shall take into account the character of the applicant, whether allowing the application may result in a breach of the law, and whether the application is in any way adverse to the public interest.[45] As Bossons and Makuch point out, the Commission tends to orient its questioning towards the applicant's criminal and driving records. Refusal of a taxi licence because of political views and previous criminal convictions by the Commission has been upheld by the courts where it was felt that the applicant's beliefs would cause him to discriminate against minority groups when serving the public.[46]

Division of power in two-tier systems
Where regional governments are in place, the province sometimes has to decide whether an upper- or lower-tier municipality is best suited to perform the licensing function. The choice is likely to differ depending on the activity in question. For instance, some businesses such as taxis, auctioneers, and fuel dealers are essentially regional in nature. Wider authority is also obviously most appropriate in an area like Metropolitan Toronto where virtually the entire area is populated without interruption. In Toronto, the population centre exceeds the Metro boundaries. With ongoing disputes occurring between Metro Toronto and Mississauga taxi drivers, it is possible that, at least in that case, one licensing authority should extend beyond Metro boundaries.

In the larger centres, for the appropriate activities, regional licensing can offer several advantages. A single licence, instead of one for each municipality, would mean greater convenience for licensed tradesmen.[47] Licensing over a larger area

44 Ontario, *Royal Commission Inquiry into Civil Rights* (McRuer Report), Report No. 1, vol. 3, Toronto, Queen's Printer, 1968, 1117
45 Bylaw 107-78
46 *Andrews* v. *Metropolitan Licensing Commission* (1980), 12, M.P.L.R. 40 (Div. Ct.)
47 See Ontario, *Municipal Licensing Discussion Paper*, 12, for a discussion of the following points.

would facilitate the geographical mobility of tradesmen by removing municipal boundaries. To the extent that this would enhance competition, costs to the consumers of the services could be reduced. Upper-tier licensing could also aid in co-ordinating regional functions such as transportation policy. The consolidation of licensing responsibilities into one office would allow the hiring of more specialized personnel. This could improve the enforcement of the various licensing provisions administered by the licensing body.

However, not all activities can be dealt with most appropriately at the regional level. For instance, in Toronto the licensing of area-wide businesses could be conducted by the upper-tier government while problems with a specific geographical focus could be left in the realm of the area municipalities.[48] Bossons and Makuch, besides arguing strenuously that municipalities should be entitled to license land uses, also propose that this be under the purview of area municipalities as zoning is now. In making this argument they acknowledge that the licensing of trades and businesses is usually best dealt with at the regional level.

The province could divide the licensing powers between upper- and lower-tier municipalities itself through the legislation governing each regional municipality. Alternatively, it could allow the regional government to pass licensing bylaws over activities which it felt best qualified to regulate. The residual licensing powers would be under the control of the area municipalities. Therefore, in the second approach, the regional municipality and not the province would determine the division of powers between the upper and lower tiers. This second approach would better fulfil the objective of increased local autonomy and flexibility than the first, but it could come at the cost of greater tension between the regional government and the area municipalities.

48 Ontario, *Royal Commission on Metropolitan Toronto (Goldenberg Report)*, Toronto, Queen's Printer, 1965, 63

2

Municipal licensing: regulation in search of a rationale

JOHN BOSSONS and S.M. MAKUCH

INTRODUCTION

Since well before Confederation, municipalities in Ontario have had powers over certain trades and businesses. For example, the Revised Statutes of Upper Canada 1859, c. 54, gave municipalities the power to license taverns, billiards parlours, victualling houses, exhibitions, places of amusement, auctioneers, hawkers, peddlers, livery stables, and cabs, and the power to pass 'such other regulations as the good of the inhabitants requires.' The authority of municipalities in this area has expanded over the years to include many other businesses such as television aerial installers, chimney sweeps, gas stations, and barber shops. In Metropolitan Toronto in recent years the number of licences issued has been over 78,000 annually.[1] Although that number has declined from a high of 82,000 in 1970,[2] it indicates that licensing has a significant and direct impact on many people who do business in the metropolitan community.

Until recently there has been no general power for municipalities to 'license, regulate or govern' businesses found in provincial legislation. As a result the municipality's ability to regulate a particular business, occupation, or persons depends on specific legislative grants of regulatory power for each business. In total, municipalities have been granted authority to regulate seventy-two specific categories of trades in the Municipal Act.[3]

The categories of trades subject to municipal licensing represent an ad hoc assortment.[4] In part, this reflects the fact that the existing grants of licensing power

1 Interview with Peter Clark, Chairman, Metropolitan Toronto Licensing Commission, 7 February 1979
2 *Review of Licensing Function in Metropolitan Toronto*, November 1977, 15
3 R.S.O. 1980, c. 302. This number is based on the author's subjective determination of categories.
4 For example, municipalities may license pet shops, hearses, boats for hire, sellers of milk and bread, taxis, body rub parlours, and plumbers.

are the result of a series of independent legislative decisions over a period of 130 years.[5] It also reflects the occasional use of such grants of licensing power as a visible means of political response to public outrage over an individual event.[6] All in all, there has been no overall examination of whether municipal licensing should be used to regulate such activities. The rationale for municipal licensing has not been examined, and its efficacy has not been evaluated in specific cases.

The government of Ontario in 1982 introduced legislation to provide municipalities with a general power to license, govern, or regulate any business.[7] While eliminating some of the obviously anachronistic features of the existing grants of licensing powers to municipalities, it would also expand municipal regulatory powers in a limited way.

This study will discuss the rationales for municipal licensing and attempt to ascertain, through an examination of the licensing process, whether the purposes of such licensing can be and are being attained. It will also seek to ascertain the effects of municipal licensing as reflected in restrictions on entry and/or increased business costs. In addition, it will discuss problems arising from the implementation of licensing, including process costs. Some alternative methods that might achieve the perceived purposes of municipal licensing with lesser costs or fewer detrimental effects will be reviewed, including provincial licensing, modifications of the current system of municipal licensing, and other techniques that might be implemented at either the provincial or municipal level.

The concrete example used is the experience of municipal licensing in Metropolitan Toronto. The example shows that the uncertainty of purpose found in provincial legislation is reflected at the municipal level, resulting in a 'hodge-podge' of regulation lacking any kind of integrated approach. Perhaps fortunately, municipal licensing has consequently had very little effect on the conduct of most businesses in Toronto. Although a general power to license may be desirable to permit flexibility, what is more important is to determine the purposes to be served by municipal regulation and the breadth of power required for that regulation.

5 The authority to regulate 72 per cent of the businesses currently subject to municipal licensing was granted prior to 1950. The present powers were granted over the period 1849–1983.
6 For example, the licensing of shoe repair and shoeshine shops was included in the Municipal Act in 1946 because of publicity relating to a young boy who was assaulted in a shoeshine shop. More recently the Act was amended to permit municipal regulation of body rub parlours and then adult entertainment parlours in response to the impact that such businesses had on certain parts of the City of Toronto.
7 Bill 11, 2nd Session, 32nd Legislature, Ontario. The bill was given second reading on 5 July 1982 and then withdrawn for further consideration. It is over five years since the province first announced on 15 April 1977 that it intended to move in this area. In the interim, several draft bills have appeared.

MUNICIPAL LICENSING POWERS

Although the Municipal Act has explictly stated what businesses or trades a municipality may regulate, it has not been at all clear about the purpose of that regulation. In other areas, such as land use planning, the nature and functions of municipal regulation are more clearly indicated in provincial statutes, and judicial decisions have used such definitions in assessing whether municipal decisions are within powers delegated to them by the province. The Municipal Act enables municipalities to 'license, regulate or govern.' The legislation states that the power to license a particular trade or calling includes the power to prohibit the carrying on of the trade or calling without a licence and thus enables municipalities to enforce a system of required licensure rather than mere certification. The Act further provides that the power to regulate a trade, calling, business, occupation, or person (with certain restrictions and exceptions) includes the right to regulate the hours of operation of businesses.[8] Such a provision itself does not indicate any clear purpose for municipal licensing.

Section 110(6) of the Act provides that the granting, refusing, or revoking of licences to any person is at the discretion of the municipal council or board of commissioners issuing the licence. This section would seem to indicate a wide authority to regulate for any purpose the municipality deems appropriate. The validity of this interpretation is strengthened by the relatively few statutory restrictions on municipal use of such licensing powers. The Act provides protection in s. 110(7) for existing businesses in that a licence cannot be refused by reason only of the location of a business where the business was carried on at that location prior to the bylaw. This provision provides a type of 'non-conforming use' for existing businesses where those businesses are in existence and being regulated only for locational reasons. Also, section 111 of the Act prohibits Council, with one exception, from conferring on any person the exclusive right of exercising any business, trade, or calling within a municipality and further prohibits a special tax on any business, calling, or trade unless authorized under the Act.

If the general sections regarding municipal licensing provide no clear indication of the purpose of that licensing, the particular provisions respecting individual businesses are no more definitive. In most sections the Act merely repeats the general words authorizing municipalities to pass bylaws for 'licensing, regulating and governing' the particular activity. For example: section 227(2) enables councils of towns, villages, and townships, and boards of commissioners of police and cities to pass bylaws for 'licensing, regulating or governing keepers of livery stables and of horses used for hire.' Section 228(1) provides similar power

8 R.S.O. 1980 c. 302, s. 110(3).

respecting salvage shops, salvage yards, second-hand goods shops, and dealers in second-hand goods. Similarly, section 230(1) enables certain municipalities to license, regulate and govern itinerant salesmen, and subsection 4 of that section provides similar powers for dealers in fruit. None of these sections, on language alone, indicates the purpose of the particular licensing power or the licensing power in general.

Some sections, it should be noted, do provide wider authority than mere licensing, regulating, and governing. Certain sections enable the setting of rates to be charged by particular businesses, as in the case of taxicabs and other vehicles for hire.[9] Municipalities are also enabled to set a limit on the number of taxicabs to be permitted within the municipality. Similarly, the numbers of and licences for billiard tables may be limited,[10] and a limit may be placed on the number of licences for body rub parlours[11] and adult entertainment parlours.[12] In some instances the regulation of hours of operation is specifically provided for, because these special provisions were not removed when the Act was amended in 1975 to provide for the regulation of hours of any business.[13] The reason for including such authority to limit numbers and set rates and hours of operation, however, is not defined in the legislation. It is clear the Legislature wished to grant such authority, but whether to regulate competition, suppress an activity, or prevent a nuisance is not clear from the words of the Act alone nor from the mere granting of that particular power.

The purposes of municipal regulation are not clearly indicated by the language of the legislation. Indeed, it would appear from the legislation that there are a multitude of possible purposes with certain outer parameters defining the extent to which such purposes may be pursued. Those purposes have to be assessed through an examination of the way in which the statute is used and of the potential benefits to be derived from municipal regulation of particular markets.

ECONOMIC RATIONALE

Licensing is one of a number of devices that may be used by government to intervene in markets to regulate the behaviour of participants. For licensing to be socially desirable two conditions must be satisfied: first, there must be some form of market failure justifying government intervention; second, licensing must be

9 Ibid., s. 227(1)
10 Ibid., s. 111(2)
11 Ibid., s. 221
12 Ibid., s. 222
13 Ibid., s. 110(3)

preferable to alternative forms of regulation. Whether these conditions are valid in the markets to which municipal licensing is applied will now be discussed.

1 Market failure

Market failure refers to a situation in which unconstrained markets do not yield an optimal allocation of resources. Such failure may be the result of any one of a number of different causes. In the markets in which municipal licensing now occurs, incomplete information about product quality is of particular importance as a source of potential market failure.

The classic example of potential market failure due to incomplete information is the used car market.[14] Buyers of used cars have limited information concerning product quality, and so predict product quality on the basis of a known or presumed distribution of quality (assuming, for example, that the best estimate of product quality is the average quality of used cars sold in previous years). Sellers on the other hand know the quality of individual used cars. Because the price of used cars depends only on the average quality of used cars normally traded (or on other statistics of the known or presumed distribution) and not on the attributes of individual cars, potential sellers of cars of above-average quality will be unable to obtain a price which realizes the benefits of the above-average quality. At the same time, owners of cars of below-average quality will face an incentive to sell. As a result, most of the used cars exchanged in the used car market will tend to be of poor quality ('lemons'). Because of this adverse selection, owners of good cars will not be able to sell their cars at a price that reflects their true value.

The market failure in this case is represented by the lack of a market in good used cars; it arises because of the inability of the owner of a good car to be able to provide the seller with reliable information as to the true quality of the car. This adverse selection problem can arise in any situation in which produce quality is variable and one side of a market has access to better information about the quality than the other.[15] Examples of such situations include the market for tradesmen, where buyers generally do not have easy access to accurate information regarding the quality of services to be provided. In such circumstances adverse selection could lead to a progressive elimination from the market of skilled tradesmen.

---

14 The discussion in this paragraph follows that in Akerlof, 'The market for lemons: qualitative uncertainty and the market mechanism,' *Quarterly Journal of Economics*, 84 (1970), 488–500.

15 As Akerlof notes (pp. 492–4) the principle of adverse selection is of particular importance in the market for insurance and is recognized as such in insurance textbooks. The general inability of persons to buy life insurance at ages above 65 is an example of market failure due to adverse selection. For a review of contributions on the adverse selection problem and its relationship to moral hazard, see Section 1.2.2 of Hirschleifer and Riley, 'The analytics of uncertainty and information: an expository survey,' *Journal of Economic Literature*, 17 (1979), 1375–1421.

The negative effects of adverse selection may be offset or ameliorated by regulatory intervention that either increases the availability to buyers of reliable information about product quality (permitting better buyer differentiation between products of differing true quality) or decreases the range of product quality. Regulation to set minimum produce standards is an example of the latter. Analysis of the need for regulation must focus on the causes of incomplete information, and in particular must explain why market forces do not cause fuller information to be generated in the absence of regulatory intervention.

There are a number of ways in which information may be generated in unregulated markets. Information is itself a product and can be produced to meet a demand. In addition, buyers' uncertainty as to product quality may be reduced by sellers' use of risk-sharing contracts (e.g. warranties) or by sellers' investments in the reputation of his brand name. The pure 'market-for-lemons' model is one in which the availability of information is independently determined; in actuality, however, the availability of information is determined by decisions of market participants. Where the information provided by sellers is incomplete, it is necessary to find reasons why independent information-providing agents do not arise in response to the potential demand for information by buyers.

In evaluating the effect of insufficient information, it is thus necessary right away to note that information, whether about product quality or anything else, is produced at a cost and is potentially traded in markets as is any other good or service.[16] The production, distribution, storage, and assessing of information all involve resource costs, but in this respect the provision of information is no different from the provision of any other good or service. To argue that intervention is socially desirable, it is necessary to show (1) that there is a market failure in the provision of information or in the provision of insurance against uncertainty caused by lack of information, (2) that regulatory intervention provides an effective means of offsetting the market failure, and (3) that the social value of the benefits thus obtained more than offsets the social costs of regulation, including both the cost of time and other resources absorbed by the regulatory process and the social costs attributable to any efficiency losses resulting from indirect side effects of regulation.[17]

Whether or not the benefits of regulatory intervention designed to reduce

16 See, for example, Stigler, 'The economics of information,' *Journal of Political Economy*, 69 (1961), 213–25.
17 These side effects may also include reduced return to entrepreneurs who might otherwise undertake to organize firms (or non-profit institutions) to provide information. In cases where regulation reduces private demand for information, one obviously cannot assume that a lack of information-distributing private agencies necessarily implies anything about whether such agencies would or would not have arisen in the absence of regulation.

uncertainty outweigh the costs of such intervention is something which can only be answered case by case. In general, regulatory intervention is socially useful only in markets for services or trades in which the market structure for some reason does not create incentives for information to be generated by private firms. In identifying features of a market which affect the provision of information, frequency of repeated contracting and the importance of reputation are primary factors on which to focus. The private return to a seller from the production of accurate information depends largely on the extent to which a 'brand image' can be made important to buyers. It is no accident that industries characterized by many small firms with few repeat sales are the primary type of business to be municipally regulated; there is little private return to a brand image in such businesses. By contrast, where repeat purchases are frequent, or where reputation may be enhanced by jointly investing in quality control and advertising, the resultant market incentives may induce at least some producers to invest in reputation.

Where product quality is variable but unregulated markets induce investments in reputation, such investments are often likely to constitute effective entry barriers. Reputation is not quickly obtained, and the resulting rents accruing to existing reputations may deter entry by new competitors.[18] Uncertainty due to incomplete information as to product quality thus can lead either to market failure in competitive markets or to an oligopolistic market structure. From this viewpoint, licensing and similar forms of regulatory intervention may be viewed as an attempt to substitute for one of the benefits of oligopolistic markets: namely, the incentive in such markets to create investments in brand images.

A potential consumer of goods or services supplied by an industry containing many suppliers would, in the absence of uncertainty concerning product quality, benefit from the competition implied by the larger number of firms. However, where it is difficult or costly in time or money to obtain information about product quality and the distribution of product prices charged by suppliers, the consumer may benefit from the potential for competition only to the extent that time or money is invested to obtain information about quality and price differences. Where such information is expensive and the frequency of use of such information is low, the amount of information generated by the market is likely to be low.[19] Where the

18 Such causes of entry-deterring barriers were discussed at length by Bain, *Barriers to New Competition*, Harvard, 1956; for a survey of the role of advertising, see Comanor and Wilson, 'The effect of advertising on competition: a survey,' *Journal of Economic Literature*, 17 (1979), 453–76.

19 Frequency in the use of information is closely related to the concept of demonstration effects used by Kotowitz and Mathewson, 'Informative advertising and welfare,' *American Economic Review*, 69 (1979), 284–94. It should be noted that the demand for information is not constant across households, and that there are economies of scale in the provision of information.

benefits of providing information cannot be appropriated by sellers (e.g. through reputation rents), it may also be difficult for independent agents to charge for providing such information. It is likely that there are economies of scale in the provision of information, so that there may be a potential for independent private agencies to be organized to provide information.[20]

However, it is important to note that such agencies are also dependent on the development of a reputation and so are subject to the same disincentives for investment as are faced by a producer. It is not much less difficult or expensive for an agency to build up a reputation than for a producer to do the same. As a result, in most competitive markets in which products of uncertain quality are sold, market failures occur that could have been ameliorated through information-enhancing regulatory intervention.[21]

In the case of the markets for skilled tradesmen, the frequency of repeat transactions with individual customers is low. In some cases where the potential transactions are larger, there is a return to producer investments in reputation through advertising jobs done for neighbours through which producer quality can be assessed. Such returns are highest in cases (e.g. painting or carpentry) in which the quality of work can be easily assessed from visible evidence. Such returns are lower in cases (e.g. plumbing or electrical work) where the quality of work is not easily assessed or where poor quality may become evident only with the passage of time. While reputation and personal references are not unimportant contributors to tradesmen's income, their importance is limited by inherent restrictions on the extent to which they can reduce uncertainty about the quality of the services provided. It is probably the inherent difficulty for most consumers of assessing the quality of services provided by tradesmen at the time that accounts for the relative paucity of private investments in tradesmen's reputations by either producers or information-providing agents.

2 Licensing vs alternative forms of regulation
Where information about quality and the distribution of prices is limited, licensing

---

20 Home-owner repair societies and consumer co-ops provide examples of ways in which household investments in information may be made more efficient; alternatively, such entities may be viewed as institutional means by which consumer organizations may be used to create brand images in atomistic markets. An obvious question is why such entities are frequently organized as consumer co-ops rather than profit-making businesses. This may occur because consumers presume that co-ops are more reliably objective. It is also noteworthy that in many cases the difference between co-ops and businesses is minimal, in that the return to the entrepreneur who organizes a consumer co-op may still be obtained as salary.

21 Cf. for example Stiglitz, 'Equilibrium in product markets with imperfect information,' *American Economic Association*, Papers and Proceedings, 69 (1979), 339–45.

may be used as a means of ensuring a minimum standard of quality.[22] However, it is necessary to ask whether licensing is a more effective means of reducing risk than other forms of regulatory intervention. Because the problem in such situations is to reduce risk (in the sense of reducing the probability of receiving highly misleading information), alternative approaches might be to require warranties (allowing contracts to be rescinded where warranties are not provided or lived up to) or to provide quality insurance funds and compel vendors to contribute to such funds. A further alternative is to attempt through legislation to assign liability for product defects to producers and to facilitate consumer litigation to recover damages.[23]

The usefulness of licensing compared to these alternatives depends partly on the nature of the informational problem and partly on market structure and the distribution of firms by size. Where producers are large and well established, the requirement that producers accept liability for differences between actual and advertised product quality can be an efficient means of increasing overall welfare in the allocation of risk.[24] However, the specification of 'quality' and adjudication of differences can be difficult and costly, so that it is important to deal with the institutional means by which costs of adjudication are determined. A simple assignment of liability to producers that is enforced through litigation will work best in a situation where product risk is concerned with low-probability events that involve significant changes in consumer wealth or human capital, such as occur in automobile safety defects. Where the effects of variations in product quality are less extreme, the returns to private enforcement of producer liability will not offset the cost of judicial action, and more informal means of adjudication are required. As will be seen below, municipal licensing provides a means for informal adjudication of contract disputes.

The usefulness of requiring warranties involves many of the same enforceability problems as with the more general assignment of liability to producers. Where the enforcement of warranties is through litigation, the costs of such litigation may make warranties ineffective except where it is profitable for producers to invest in brand images. Where producers are generally small, where frequency of contact

---

22 The effect of licensing is not necessarily beneficial (even gross of costs) and may be perverse. If licensing advertises standards which are not enforced, if repeat sales are infrequent (as is the case with licensed tradesmen), and if quality is difficult to perceive prior to a transaction, then licensing may create misperceptions which induce less search by consumers and hence lower welfare.

23 It should be underlined that these alternatives are not mutually exclusive.

24 It should be noted that the requirement of warranties is an attempt to shift liability from the consumer to the producer. With imperfect information it can be shown that such a shift can increase welfare. Cf. Epple and Raviv, 'Product safety: liability rules, market structure, and imperfect information,' *American Economic Review*, 68 (1978), 80–95.

between producers and consumers is low, and where information about product quality is costly, investments in brand images are unlikely to be profitable.

The differences in market structure will also affect the utility of product warranties as a means of dealing with product risk. Where firms are generally small, the risk of bankruptcy or business termination may be sufficiently high to make warranties ineffective. While at first sight this problem may seem capable of solution through requiring producers to provide a deficiency fund for the payment of warranties or damages for which bankrupt producers are liable, the institution of such insurance leads to further problems of moral hazard and cross-subsidization.[25] The moral hazard problem arises from the incentive such insurance offers to high-risk producers; even without such incentives, it would be difficult to design such insurance so that low-risk producers would not be forced to subsidize high-risk producers. Such problems may be reduced through using licensing institutions as a means of attempting to establish lower limits on product quality.

In summary, licensing is only one means of regulatory intervention, and its function may in many cases be achieved through other devices such as liability assignments and producers insurance. Licensing is likely to be most useful in industries where there are no economies of scale and entry barriers are low (so that such industries are characterized both by a large number of small firms and by a high frequency of firm turnover), where the potential range of product quality is wide, and where information about product quality is costly or unreliable. It is no accident that such circumstances apply to many of the trades currently subject to licensing controls.

Licensing may also be a useful complement to other forms of regulation used to establish minimum quality standards. For example, it may be used to enforce the provision of warranties through providing a means for excluding vendors from the market who do not conform to the requirements of warranty or insurance regulation.

One of the key attributes of licensing is that the vendor's possession of a licence to do business is potentially an important piece of information for a consumer.

Other objectives of municipal licensing
In addition to regulatory intervention to reduce uncertainty regarding product quality, there are a number of other reasons for municipal licensing. These include the assurance of probity in transactions (an extension of anti-fraud law), the

25 In addition, it should be noted that the establishment of mandatory insurance schemes causes a 'free rider' problem that often leads to industry pressure for licensing in order to try to reduce the costs of insurance. Travel agents in Ontario provide a current case study in this respect.

regulation of externalities, the regulation of public morality, general market regulation, and supplementation of other legislation.

1 Assuring probity

Ensuring the honesty of suppliers of goods and services is closely allied to the problems of externalities and information. As noted earlier, consumers are often unable to judge the quality of work done or to choose a good supplier. In addition, consumers are also often unable to obtain redress if they are victimized by unscrupulous or negligent vendors. Licensing is a means of establishing minimum standards of probity and competency, using the threat of revocation of licences to provide a deterrent to 'shady dealing.' In effect, this latter use of licensing is an extension of consumer protection provisions in the Criminal Code which may be otherwise difficult to enforce.

The importance of this objective from an allocative viewpoint is due to the effect of standards of honesty upon the objectivity of information on product quality (and on price/quality tradeoffs) provided by individual producers.

2 Externalities

Externalities may arise in connection with the operation of many businesses.[26] Local externalities may partly be dealt with through the use of zoning bylaws.[27] However, zoning bylaws are meant to provide 'permanent' designations for land use that are independent of user performance, and their use is restricted by legal interpretation to such designation. Nevertheless, the nature and extent of local externalities may be critically dependent on aspects of user performance, including such seemingly minor items as the disposition of garbage, snow removal, etc. Licensing provides a means by which performance standards may be set and uses made conditional on meeting such standards.

The regulation of performance may be a useful substitute for intervention through the use of municipal zoning power to restrict land uses. Where externalities are related to user performance, locally varying performance standards for the operation of different types of business can provide a type of 'performance zoning' which deals more directly with the reasons for municipal land use control than the

26 Externalities or third-party effects occur when some of the costs of producing goods and services are not borne by the producing business or when some benefits of goods or services do not accrue to consumers who purchase them. Negative externalities may cause adverse effects on neighbouring uses and property values or adversely affect third parties who are physically injured by accidents occurring as a result of defects in workmanship.
27 Cf. Bossons, *Reforming Planning in Ontario: Strengthening the Municipal Role* (Ontario Economic Council, 1978), chap. 2.

mere designation of restricted use categories. For example, in regulating commercial uses in land adjacent to residential areas, the most relevant concerns are the hours of operations, noise standards, the control of odours emitted, and other highly specific aspects of user performance. The direct regulation of such matters through licensing may permit less restrictive municipal zoning.

Curiously, the potential for use of municipal licensing as an adjunct to the zoning bylaw has been very little utilized, partly because of restrictions on the ways in which municipal licensing powers may be used.[28] Nevertheless, some aspects of current municipal licensing do reflect this use. Moreover, municipalities' use of licensing powers might be expanded in this direction if existing restrictions on their powers to license were removed or reduced.

Third-party effects of defective workmanship are a different type of externality, which may justify certain types of licensing, particularly in the building trades. In this case, reduction of uncertainty with respect to product quality is assumed to be socially beneficial because of the consequent avoidance of social and / or private third-party costs arising from accidents resulting from defective products. As in other areas, an important feature of the rationale for the use of licensing for this purpose is the role it can play as part of a package of regulatory intervention including the establishment of quality standards (e.g. building codes), enforcement of standards through inspection, and possibly also the establishment of warranty and / or insurance schemes. The role of licensing in such packages may be primarily to enhance the effectiveness of other regulatory devices through which minimal standards may be achieved.

The usefulness of licensing as a means of dealing with safety considerations is largely dependent on the effectiveness of enforcement. If producers are organized in relatively small units, as in many of the building trades, producer liability is effectively limited by the relatively high chance of bankruptcy (particularly on the part of high-risk producers). While compulsory producer liability insurance may be viewed as a method by which bankruptcy risk may be eliminated, the moral hazard arising from the incentives implicit in such insurance introduces a potential disequilibrium. Licensing may consequently be necessary to reduce the potential moral hazard.

3 Regulation of public morality

Issues of public morality or social values have often been dealt with through the licensing mechanisms. The recent provision of authority to regulate body rub

---

28 In particular, judicial interpretation of the Municipal Act has provided that licensing cannot be used as a form of zoning. This has the side effect of causing zoning designations to be made more restrictive than might otherwise be the case, forcing, for example, restaurants to be forbidden in some areas where the principal objective is to restrict hours of operation.

parlours and adult entertainment parlours is in part an attempt to restrict such activities because they are viewed as socially undesirable or morally wrong. That such objectives have no economic content does not diminish their importance.

4 General market regulation

Licensing can be used for regulating the market in a more general way to restrict competition or to prevent abuses as a result of unequal bargaining power. It is often presumed by regulators that without some form of licensing to create 'property rights' in certain activities such as cab driving, competition in the industry might well result in a situation where so many persons are providing a service that no one could earn an adequate wage. The perceived rationale is presumably similar to that advanced for minimum-wage legislation. Beyond that, there seems also to be some presumption that low wages in certain industries may cause an increase in criminal activities through reducing the opportunity cost of investing time in crime.[29]

Regardless of the validity of the foregoing presumptions, it is a curious fact that, in licensing activities where entry is regulated, wages are not subject to regulation. The primary economic effects of regulating taxicabs are in reducing the availability of taxi services and increasing the market value of taxicab licences. The regulation of conditions of employment is also not within the purview of taxicab licensing. Consequently, it would be difficult to conclude that taxicab licensing has any effect on the wages of taxi drivers other than to lower the demand for their services through restricting the use of cabs.

A more important aspect of market regulation is the effect on the demand for licensing arising from the creation of property rights. Here it is noteworthy that the creation of increased market values of semi-tradeable licences is viewed by some regulators as a means by which pension rights may be created for driver / owners. This is but one aspect of the fact that, having used licensing as a means of creating property rights, it is difficult to find politically acceptable means of eliminating such rights.

5 A supplement to other legislation

Municipal licensing may serve to assist in the enforcement of other legislation. Municipalities have other regulatory provisions to deal with externalities. The use of zoning bylaws and public health regulations are examples of regulations dealing with externalities, although approaching from the demand side rather than the supply side. The provincial level of government in Ontario deals with externalities

---

29 Obviously such presumptions (like all attempts to legislate minimum wages) ignore the effects of minimum-wage rules on the employability of low-skill workers. The opportunity cost of investing time in criminal activities is zero for a person who is not employable at minimum wages.

through such legislation as the Ontario Building Code and the Liquor Licence Act and with informational problems in business through the Consumers Protection Act and the Business Practices Act. The federal government seeks to deal with informational problems by prohibiting fraud in the Criminal Code. It deals with morality in the Code as well. Furthermore, the Combines Investigation Act attempts to deal with general market regulation. There are therefore many other legal tools that can be used to achieve the same purposes of municipal licensing. At the municipal level, all these purposes are brought together for regulation through the use of one technique – that of licensing. More important, the power to revoke licences of businesses which are in violation of other regulations may be used as a means by which compliance with these other regulations may be encouraged.

Redistributive sources of demand for municipal regulation
Two additional motivations for advocating such regulation are discussed in this section: (1) its potential use by regulated firms as a means of reducing competition, and (2) its use as a placebo by politicians. Both of these are purely redistributive, in that neither is concerned with improvements in allocative efficiency.

The sources of political pressures underlying decisions to introduce or expand municipal regulations are useful to examine, if only to ascertain whether the potential purposes listed above are in fact the real objectives of the regulatory intervention.

1 Regulation to redistribute wealth
A growing literature has focused on the redistributing effects of government regulation, emphasizing that its principal economic effect on regulated individuals or businesses may be to reduce competition, thus causing a government-induced redistribution of wealth in favour of the regulated firms.[30] In simplistic versions of this view, it is the regulated businesses or firms that are the beneficiaries of regulation and are therefore the chief sources of political support for such regulation. In this view, regulation simply transfers wealth from consumers to the regulated producers.[31] In more complex versions of this view, the regulated firms are, along with consumers, among the principal beneficiaries of regulation and so

30 See, for example, the discussion of participants' interests in Trebilcock, Waverman, and Prichard, 'Markets for regulation: implications for performance standards and institutional design,' in *Government Regulation: Issues and Alternatives*, Ontario Economic Council, 1978, 11–66.
31 In this model, politicians may also benefit through explicit bribery or through receiving services that contribute to subsequent electoral success.

are an important but not dominating member of the political coalition supporting regulation.

It should be emphasized that in some cases the redistributive effects of regulation may be primarily among producers (rather than from consumers to producers), and that such redistributive transfers may be accompanied by increases in consumer welfare where the effect of reducing competition is to increase the provision of information. Such cases can arise where there is a significant range in product quality and where entry barriers may provide increased returns to investments in product quality or information dissemination. As noted previously, the conventional wisdom regarding the optimality of unlimited competition can provide misleading policy prescriptions when applied to situations characterized by imperfect and costly information.

In most areas in which municipal licensing is actively used (other than taxicabs and cartage), it is doubtful that licensing has significant redistributive effects. This is because, with the exception of the taxicab and cartage industries, municipal licensing does not generally create any significant entry barriers. In areas such as licensing building trades, the major entry barriers consist of provincial certification requirements; any effect of municipal licensing on numbers is thus primarily through the extent to which it increases the effective enforcement of provincial standards. In such areas, the major effects of municipal licensing are not redistributive even though any attempt at maintenance of minimum standards of competence and honesty will necessarily have some redistributive effect.

An analysis of recent extensions of licensing powers of Metropolitan Toronto and of proposed further extensions suggests that, with one exception, it is not the businesses to be regulated which seek municipal licensing. A recent extension of licensing standards for pet shops was, for example, primarily the result of pressures from the Humane Society and other animal lovers. There has been pressure in recent years to obtain powers to license house painters, but such pressure is primarily from consumer complaints. The one example of firms seeking regulation is in the auto-towing industry, where an association of larger firms has actively lobbied for regulations that would discourage 'unethical' competition by smaller firms.[32] Even here, the awareness by municipal legislators of the obvious self-

32 The bylaw finally enacted to regulate tow-trucks did not control the use of CB radios by which small independent operators overheard police reports of accidents and arrived at the scene of accidents before the trucks of large firms whom the police requested to come to the scene. The major impetus for regulation was from larger firms to control the use of radios to preclude such competition. There has been lobbying by the Electrical Contractors Association of Ontario and the Mechanical Contractors Association of Ontario to maintain the present role of municipal licensing in their respective trades.

interest motivating these firms' advocacy of regulation would indicate the necessity of being able to find some purpose other than self-interest to provide at least a rationale for regulation.[33]

In general, the catalogue of purposes described in the previous section includes what seem to be the major objectives of most uses of municipal licensing. Even in the case of taxicabs, where the redistributive impact of licensing is substantial, it is clear that the activities of the Metro Licensing Commission are primarily geared to implementing regulatory objectives other than the regulation of numbers and fees. Were taxicab licensing changed by allowing free entry of any taxicab meeting minimum standards, such activities – and the purposes they serve – would be little changed.

2 Regulation as placebo

An additional motivation for regulatory initiatives is what cynically might be termed its use as a placebo. In situations where there is substantial public concern over some insoluble issue, the political attractiveness of undertaking some tangible initiative that seemingly responds to the issue is considerable. In such circumstances, an ideal political response may be to impose regulation, which is known to be reasonably ineffective, since such a response may on the one hand satisfy the need for tangible action and on the other hand not result in undesirable restrictions of individual liberties.

To some extent extensions of municipal licensing powers may have been used for this purpose, particularly when such powers have been granted to deal with moral issues. As is shown later, the effectiveness of municipal licensing has been limited. Municipal licensing is thus an obvious instrument to turn to in situations where a placebo is required.

Nevertheless it would be unrealistic to assume that either its legislative extensions or its functioning is very largely the result of its use in this way. What is more realistic is to recognize that some extensions to municipal licensing powers were motivated by the need to find a tangible means of responding to public outrage over a particular event, and that in such cases it should not be surprising to find that such powers are not in fact utilized.[34] In this respect, placebo powers are indistinguishable from historical anachronisms such as the power to regulate livery stables; both clutter up municipal statutes and are in fact vestigial and irrelevant. Our analysis of

---

33 Beyond this, the extent to which provincial standards themselves restrict numbers depends on the level of such standards and also on the extent to which vocational training is available to assist potential entrants to meet such standards.

34 The regulation of shoeshine businesses provides a clear example. Motivated by a 1946 crime committed against a shoeshine boy, it remains an element of both provincial statute and municipal bylaws. However, the provisions of the Metro bylaw are not enforced.

licensing will be restricted to those applications of municipal licensing in which the Metro Toronto Licensing Commission is active.

IMPLEMENTATION

The provisions of municipal bylaws
An examination of licensing provisions indicates that the purposes outlined above can all be discovered in current uses of municipal licensing. Those provisions, however, do not result in an integrated or clear system of regulation.

1 Regulating competency and product quality
Market failures caused by informational and externality problems can be dealt with to some extent by the regulation of the competency of persons providing services and by the establishment of minimum quality standards. In the area of municipal licensing, competency requirements are often shared between the provincial and municipal governments. Generally, where there is a requirement for provincial certification as in the case of driving school instructors or barbers, the municipality does not require further proof of competency. In other cases, for example tradesmen such as plumbers and electricians, there are both provincial and municipal competency requirements.[35] The municipal licensing with respect to tradesmen involves a competency test at the time of application for a licence. The test is a verbal one conducted by a board consisting of at least one person from the municipal building inspection department, one person from the Provincial Institute of Trade, and one person who practises the particular trade. All tradesmen's examining boards are structured in a similar way.

Although the requirements for testing at two levels of government would appear to be redundant,[36] municipal testing may serve to reflect different skill requirements in different municipalities. For example, it is suggested that because of the number of high-rise buildings in Toronto there is a need for more sophisticated skills in plumbing and electricity than in other parts of Ontario. In addition, local hydro commission requirements may vary from municipality to municipality. The licensing commission also attempts to ensure competency in certain

35 See the Apprenticeship and Tradesmen's Qualification Act, R.S.O. 1980 c. 24 and Bylaw 107-78 Schedule 13, re: electrical contractor and master electricians, and Schedule 23, re: plumbing contractors, plumbers and master plumbers.
36 This is particularly true since there is one Building Code for the whole province. See the Ontario Building Code Act, R.S.O. 1980, c. 51.

aspects of taxi driving, even providing training in its own school to ensure that cab drivers have a detailed knowledge of the geography of Metropolitan Toronto.[37]

An attempt to regulate the quality of goods and services can also be seen in the municipal bylaw. The provisions requiring information on the driving records of taxi and cartage drivers can be seen as an attempt to deal with the problem of quality of service on the basis that a bad driving record may indicate poor service. Requirements regarding the mechanical inspection and fitness of vehicles may be similarly interpreted.

Some of the provisions of licensing bylaws seem primarily to be expressions of hope. A common provision for cab drivers and school bus drivers, as well as for adult entertainment parlour operators and employees, is that they be 'properly dressed, neat and clean and civil and well behaved' while on duty. The bylaw also provides, with respect to cabs, that 'no owner or driver shall knowingly mislead or deceive any person as to the location of any place.' With respect to cartage vehicles there is a similar provision that drivers shall take the most direct travelled route to the point of destination and return to the point of origin in the most expedient manner. School driver instructors are prohibited from teaching more than one pupil at a time. Body rub and adult entertainment parlours must provide clean towels, washing facilities, and a place for the safe-keeping of valuables. Barbers must have rolls of white paper on chairs, use clean neck bands, and not use caustic or styptic pencils or alum.[38] Such regulations may be interpreted either as a general expression of desirable virtues or as providing excuses for revocation of licenses in cases where such revocation is desired for other reasons.

In general, it appears that the function of municipal licensing (at least in Metro Toronto) is to monitor standards rather than to determine required standards in new entrants. In this respect the use of municipal licensing as an adjunct to provincial entry regulation would appear to be an appropriate division of responsibility.

2 Assuring probity

Because of the dependence of consumers on producers for information about product quality, the objective of increasing the likelihood of accurate representations as to quality on the part of the producer has been pursued in Metropolitan Toronto in two ways: first, by attempting to screen applicants for licences; second, by providing an extra-legal channel in dealing with consumer complaints.[39]

Application forms for all licences request information as to breaches of the

---

37 Interview with Mr Neville, Director, Metropolitan Toronto Licensing Commission, 20 February 1979
38 Bylaw No. 107-78, Schedule 4
39 The second of these two implementation techniques is dealt with together with enforcement problems below.

Criminal Code and the applicant's licensing history. (This is the major information received by the Metropolitan Toronto Licensing Commission regarding any applicant. The Commission is a body appointed by Metropolitan Toronto Council to administer its licensing bylaw.) This information is requested because the licensing bylaw provides that if, upon investigation of an applicant, there is no reason to believe the applicant's character may not be good, or that the carrying on of the trade, calling, business, or occupation may result in a breach of law or in any way be adverse to the public interest, a licence may be issued by an issuing supervisor of the Commission.[40] Aside from requirements of competency which arise in a few trades, the main concern of the issuing supervisor is the applicant's criminal and driving record (where the latter is relevant to the occupation of the applicant as in the case of cab drivers, cartage drivers, driving instructors, and school bus drivers). Section 10 of the bylaw states that where there is a refusal of an application, the applicant may have a public hearing before the Commission. Under this section, the Commission is to take into account 'the character of the applicant, the question of whether the carrying on of the said trade, call, business or occupation, may result in a breach of the law or may be in any way adverse to the public interest and any other matter which the Commission is authorized by law to consider upon such application.' Once again, given the application form, the concern of the Commission in such hearings is the criminal and / or driving records of the applicant.

This approach is reflected in the conduct for hearings of the Commission. Its questioning relates almost exclusively to the criminal and / or driving records of applicants. The Commission, it can therefore be argued, is seeking out information on applicants as a method of discerning the appropriateness of their being trusted by the public. The criminal record is the standard used in this respect and is seen as an indication of whether the applicant will take advantage of the public's lack of information in the provision of services. When the record is recent (within the past five years) and when the crime may relate to the particular occupation, these facts are taken into account in the granting of a licence. For example, theft or fraud convictions are considered relevant in the cartage and insulation installers' business. Indecent assault of a minor would be a relevant concern with respect to a school bus driver as would a conviction for assault, for trafficking in drugs, or general traffic offence convictions for a cab drivers' licence. In all of these cases the Commission seeks out and, by agreement, easily obtains from the police department information to which the public would not otherwise have easy access regarding particular individuals engaged in businesses.

The difficulty and costs of each member of the public seeking such information

---

40 Municipality of Metropolitan Toronto Bylaw No. 107-78 as amended, s. 6

would be high for most individuals. Moreover, it could represent an unacceptable loss of privacy if such information were to be easily available to the public. Thus the Commission may serve as a screening agent, performing this task once for all members of the community. The problems of maintaining privacy standards are lessened through such data being available only to Commission officials and the applicant concerned.

The role of municipal licensing as a substitute for private information can be further supported by the view that the businesses that are being licensed are generally not well known with brand names, established reputations, and a vested interest in supplying accurate information about themselves to the public. Many of the businesses regulated can be described as small and local and as providing services at an individual's home. It is a rare occasion that Eaton's or Dominion Stores has need to appear before the Commission. Indeed, each of those companies has only appeared once and both times under very special circumstances.[41]

The licensing commission can be seen as akin to an employer who has a reputation to protect and is therefore concerned about the trustworthiness of his employees. The Commission at its hearings screens applicants to a large extent as if they were applicants for jobs. The criminal record is used as a rough indicator of whether they can be trusted in their relationship with the public when members of the public have little knowledge or information regarding the services being provided. The Commission goes beyond the criminal and driving records however, and also on occasion seeks to 'get a feel' for the character of the applicant in order to further determine if he can be trusted. The questions 'What do you do for a living,' 'Do you have a drinking problem,' and 'Are you happily married' are all ones that the Commission has put to applicants. It can be argued that the relevance of such questions to the ability to install insulation or drive a cab is tenuous. But seen as an attempt to determine whether the particular applicant can be trusted to deal with consumers fairly, given the information gap, the questions seem more sensible.

The details of the Metropolitan Toronto bylaw with respect to such activities as taxicab drivers, cartage drivers, and driving schools also reflect a concern with information problems.[42] They require the posting of tariffs in a prescribed form along with the name of the individual supplying the service and the maintenance of invoices, receipts, and accounts. It therefore can be argued that consumers have at the very least an opportunity to become informed of the costs of those services and if a dispute arises can rely on the receipts and accounts to reflect the actual goods

41 Interview with George Rust-D'Eye, Solicitor for the Metropolitan Toronto Licensing Commission, 12 February 1979
42 Bylaw No. 107-78 as amended. Schedule 8 deals with taxicab drivers and owners. Schedule 9 deals with cartage drivers and owners and Schedule 12 deals with driving schools.

and services provided. With respect to building renovators a standard form contract is required which includes information as to price and to consumer rights under the Consumer Protection Act.[43] These requirements, along with the general requirement of registration with the Commission, may also help deter any provider of goods or services who might consider abusing his trust and taking advantage of an information gap. These requirements, it is suggested, facilitate the screening out of such businessmen.

3 Externalities

While the provisions of the licensing bylaw may serve the goal of overcoming information problems in many cases, as noted earlier they may also attempt to deal with externalities.

The most obvious form of externality is a nuisance. In the case of body rub parlours, adult entertainment parlours, public address systems, public garages, and refreshment vehicles, one can see in the provisions of the municipal bylaw an attempt to prevent part of the costs of the activity from being borne by third parties.[44] The bylaw regulating body rub parlours addresses the external appearances and signs advertising the premises. Section 23(1) of Schedule 36 to Bylaw No. 107-78 provides that no person or operator shall 'in any way or by any means advertise a body rub parlour ... by any means or by any forms whatsoever except as specifically permitted by this bylaw.' The same section allows for one non-illuminated sign not more than 0.19 square metres in size, with lettering no more than eight centimetres in depth relating to the legal name of the owner, the name of the business, the telephone number, and address of the parlour. No other letters, marks, painting, contrasting colours, symbols, logo or any other mark whatsoever on the signs, and no other signs of identification for the parlour are permitted. The purpose of this provision, it can be argued, is to limit the effect that the appearance of such establishments may have on neighbourhoods and property values. The same purpose can be seen in a provision in the bylaw limiting the number of such establishments to eighteen in the City of Toronto and seven in the rest of Metropolitan Toronto. Indeed, much of the public concern respecting such establishments has been because of the deterioration of neighbourhoods.

Concerns over the number and spacing of land uses with negative externalities are frequent, but not usually easily handled. For example, there may be concern over the number of restaurants in a commercial area bordering a residential area, but this is not a permissible reason for denying a licence, since licences cannot be

43 R.S.O. 1980 c. 87
44 Bylaw No. 107-78 as amended, Schedule 24 deals with public address systems; Schedule 36 deals with body rub parlours; Schedule 25 deals with public garages; and Schedule 27 deals with refreshment vehicles.

denied by reason of the location of the business. At the same time, the number and spacing of restaurants cannot be dealt with through the zoning bylaw, which may only define potential uses unconditionally and cannot make permitted uses on one commercial property conditional on current or future uses of a neighbouring commercial property. Provincial legislative definitions of licensing and zoning powers (together with judicial interpretations thereof) have made both of these powers ineffective in dealing with these aspects of local externalities.

Regulating the hours of such establishments and the hours of use of public address systems also reflects an attempt to limit externalities in terms of traffic and noise. Similarly, the regulation of public garages and refreshment vehicles seems to reflect attempts to deal with externalities. The bylaw dealing with garages regulates the storage of cars and wrecks, removal of snow on sidewalks, and the display of tires and auto parts.[45] In the case of refreshment vehicles, the stopping of such vehicles on streets close to corners at certain times is regulated, primarily in order to prevent traffic congestion.

Although the use of regulations to prevent externalities in the sense of public nuisances can be found in bylaws, there is also an attempt to prevent externalities resulting from injury to individuals not party to a contract arising out of inferior workmanship. In the case of trades the Commission has set up a board of examiners to ensure a minimum competency in those trades. In the case of taxis, the cartage business, school bus drivers, and driving school instructors,[46] the bylaw provides for minimum levels of public liability insurance and certain competency requirements. Such provisions are an attempt to prevent inferior provision of services which might result in injury to third parties and to ensure that where such injury occurs it will be borne by the business through insurance.

4 Public morality

The use of municipal regulation to deal with public morality is not a recent phenomenon. The introduction of controls over bagatelle and billiard halls was in part an attempt to curtail certain undesirable social activities. The hours of those establishments are still regulated, although the numbers are not.[47] The major emphasis in the area of public morality more recently has concerned body rub and adult entertainment parlours. In addition, the municipality has recently passed an amendment to its bylaw to prohibit nudity on the part of serving persons in eating or drinking establishments.[48] The latter appears to be more important than the regulation of body rub parlours at the present time, if only because of the

45 Bylaw No. 107-78 as amended, Schedule 25
46 Bylaw No. 107-78, Schedules 8 and 8A as amended
47 Bylaw No. 107-78, Schedule 5
48 Bylaw No. 107-78, s. 14a, added by bylaw 58-79

successful use of the legislation to force objectionable body rub parlours out of business.[49] The fees for body rub and adult entertainment parlours ($3300 for the ownership and operation of body rub parlours or adult entertainment parlours) are the highest fees charged for any licence and serve to discourage such activity because it is deemed offensive to the public taste. The bylaw prohibits owners, operators, and customers who are under eighteen years of age. It prohibits the provision of any other 'services' than body rubs in body rub parlours and only allows 'services and goods' approved by the Commission to be provided in adult entertainment parlours. Furthermore, it prohibits the construction or equipment of such establishments so as to interfere with or prevent the enforcement of the bylaw. Locking devices on internal doors, for example, are prohibited. These provisions are an attempt to ensure that action can be easily taken to control and restrict such establishments and suppress any 'undesirable' conduct. In eating and drinking establishments the bylaw requires that opaque clothing must be worn over the breasts of women, and the 'pubic, perineal, and perianal areas and buttocks' of all 'serving persons.' Such provisions appear to have little rationale except the suppression of morally offensive conduct, though this rationale is of obvious political importance in that there was some public demand to control such activity.

5 Market price regulation

Municipal bylaws dealing with the regulation of market prices occur in the licensing of the taxicab and cartage businesses. The stated purpose of this regulation is to ensure that 'undue' competition does not result in an inability on the part of the members of the licensed business to generate an adequate income for themselves. A further concern stated by regulations is a fear that without regulation there would be cut-throat competition resulting not only in low wages but also in individuals turning to dishonest activities to compensate for their low wages.[50] The bylaw respecting taxicabs clearly reflects this concern and attempts to deal with it. The provisions of Section 61 of schedule 8 of the bylaw provide for the setting of a limit on the number of taxicab owners' licences in order to restrict entry to the business and prevent the problems referred to above. The bylaw further provides for the issuing of such licences on the basis of seniority or placement on a list. The bylaw also sets out a tariff that must be followed in charging for services. A tariff is also set out for the cartage industry to ensure the health of that business. With respect to taxicabs, there is also detailed regulation of the use of cab stands and the solicitation of passengers in a further attempt to regulate competition.

49 In 1977 there was only one body rub parlour licensed in Metropolitan Toronto. See Review of the Licensing Function in Metropolitan Toronto, November 1977, p. 51.
50 Interview with Mr Neville

The taxicab and cartage business seem unusual in this respect. However, there are also other limited examples of such regulation for the benefit of employees. The bylaw regulating travelling shows such as circuses has provisions to ensure employees are adequately covered by workmen's compensation[51] and seem to represent an attempt to deal with unequal bargaining power between employers and employees. Certain provisions to ensure adequate ventilation in the operation of cars in public garages have a similar objective.

6 Municipal Revenue

At one time licence fees may have served as a source of general municipal revenue. However, revenue from licence fees generally does not exceed administrative costs; where it does, net licensing revenues are an insignificant portion of municipal revenues.

It may seem appropriate to limit licence fees to administrative and enforcement costs, but it is more correct to say that, at a minimum, licence fees should cover such costs. In most cases the benefits of licensing accrue primarily to consumers, to whom the costs of licence fees can be expected to be shifted. Moreover, where entry is restricted by licences, it would be most equitable to sell the licences at public auction.

Having said this, it should also be noted that municipal licensing provides several means by which the administration of municipal business taxes may be made more effective. One way in which this occurs is through providing a record of businesses which may be assessed for business tax. A second way is providing for a means of facilitating the collection of taxes (equivalent to what would be paid under normal business tax assessment procedures) from short-term 'itinerant' businesses that might otherwise be able to avoid paying business tax. In some circumstances the easiest way of levying such supplementary taxes may be through consolidating them with licence fees; alternatively, prepayment of such taxes to local municipalities may be a condition for receipt of a licence.

Municipal licensing as an adjunct to other regulation

Municipal licensing can be described as a regulating device that has varying rationales and is utilized to deal with problems as they arise. This in turn is reflected in the fact that municipal licensing also is used as a supplementary enforcement tool for other provincial and federal legislation.

51 Bylaw No. 107-78, Schedule 14

1 Criminal law

The one Act of the federal government to which licensing is an important adjunct is the Criminal Code.[52] This is reflected not only in the fact that licensing was until recently in Metropolitan Toronto (and still is in many municipalities) conducted by the Police Commission but also in the major requirement of application forms for the applicants' criminal record. The Commission as noted earlier has an agreement with the Police Commission to receive the recent criminal record of all applicants. It should be noted that use of licensing profoundly alters the nature of regulation through a criminal law process. The criminal law process acts retroactively, only after a crime has been committed. Moreover, in the Criminal Code only the act for which the accused is charged is relevant to the court.[53]

The retrospective nature of criminal prosecution and its strict rules of evidence and proof necessarily reduces the extent to which the Criminal Code serves as a protection for potential victims of crimes. The rate of recidivism in Canada's penal institutions is high, so that information on an individual's criminal record can serve as a prediction of the likelihood of future commission of crimes. Nevertheless, most individuals do not have knowledge of the criminal records of those around them and do not know how to obtain such information.

Municipal licensing therefore can be seen as a supplement to the Criminal Code and the protection it offers. The most obvious difference between municipal licensing and the Criminal Code is the prospective application of the former. Unlike criminal proceedings, licensing does not merely look backward to see if an applicant has done a certain act, but seeks to judge if an applicant is likely to do certain acts in the future. Unlike criminal proceedings it makes its judgment using information on all previous convictions and does not direct itself merely to whether the applicant has committed one particular act. Moreover, because the applicant must show why he should be granted a licence or why his licence should not be revoked under a licensing requirement, the onus of the Criminal Code is reversed in municipal licensing.[54] As an example, Norm's Open Kitchen, a restaurant notorious for its use by prostitutes and pimps, was closed through revocation of a licence even though no crime could be shown or presumed.[55] By supplementing the Code in this way, licensing can also be seen as strengthening the deterrent

---

52 R.S.C. 1970 c. c-34
53 There are some exceptional circumstances when a previous record would be relevant. It could be admitted to show the identity of the person who committed the crime or to counter evidence of good character brought by the accused.
54 G. Rust-D'Eye, *Discretion Not Open to Question*, unpublished, p. 18. See also *Re Szabo and Metropolitan Licensing Commission*, [1963] 2 O.R. 426 (H.C.J.).
55 *Discretion Not Open to Question*, p. 19

aspect of the criminal law and, most importantly, as attempting to make the criminal law and the Code more useful in dealing with informational problems.

There are obvious drawbacks to this use of information on criminal records; these are discussed below.

2 Other municipal regulation

Other legislation is supplemented as well by municipal regulation. The licensing bylaw is used to enforce the local public health bylaw because under the Public Health Act,[56] municipalities have no authority to close restaurants in breach of the Act or bylaws passed under it. Licensing is used to supplement the zoning power. Although zoning powers cannot be exercised directly through the licensing power,[57] licences may not be granted to any establishment which would operate in contravention of a zoning bylaw. Before a licence is granted for any business in Metropolitan Toronto, for example, the area municipality is contacted to ensure compliance with local zoning bylaws.[58] In this way, zoning bylaw inspection is facilitated, because changes may be made to premises or businesses opened without the need of a building permit. In addition, the enforcement of the Ontario Building Code[59] is a municipal responsibility, and the licensing bylaw is used to facilitate the enforcement of the Code; contractors, electricians, and plumbers who are in constant breach of the Code may have their licenses revoked. Local hydro commission regulations and the provisions of the Fire Marshal's Act[60] are enforced in the same way but by local hydro and local fire department inspectors.

The use of licensing to facilitate the enforcement of other municipal regulation is a reflection of a wider patchwork of delegated authority in other areas of municipal jurisdiction. In such areas as public health and planning, the municipality has limited powers of enforcement, mainly the use of criminal proceedings, and licensing is used to fill that gap. The limited delegation of authority can be seen as an attempt to limit the authority granted to municipalities in order to prevent abuses in the use of that power. The result, however, is an incoherent system of local regulation in which licensing is used in an attempt to remedy inadequacies in the authority granted.

The problems arising from inadequate municipal powers of enforcement include limitations on both powers of inspection and on the sanctions that may be imposed where municipal bylaws are violated. While an obvious alternative to the use of municipal licensing as a subtitute enforcement device is to permit more

56 R.S.O. 1980 c. 409
57 *R. v. Donald B. Allen* (1975) 65 11 O.R. (2d) 271. D.L.R. (3rd) 599 (Div. Ct.)
58 *Supra* note 37
59 R.S.O. 1980, c. 51 s. 3
60 R.S.O. 1980, c. 166

effective direct regulation, a more adequate delegation of powers to municipalities is inhibited both by political constraints and by the traditional reluctance of the courts to impose significant penalties on individuals or firms that violate municipal bylaws.

It would be productive, particularly in larger municipalities, to delegate additional enforcement powers to municipalities in the areas of planning and public health. Doing so would require a careful definition of individual's rights of appeal so that suitable checks are placed on the arbitrary exercise of municipal power. Nevertheless, it would clearly be preferable to introduce necessary checks and balances by ensuring the protection of individual rights than, as at present, by simply ensuring that municipal regulation is ineffective.

Providing a more satisfactory definition of municipal regulatory and enforcement powers would reduce the need to rely on municipal licensing powers as a substitute for direct enforcement. It may still then be useful to use licensing powers as a supplement to direct regulation, but the supplementary role of municipal licensing could then be directed more at ensuring that individual buyers are not subjected to the costs of replacing work which contravenes municipal regulations as a result of contractors' short cuts.

3 Provincial consumer protection legislation

The Ontario government has passed both the Consumer Protection Act[61] and the Business Practices Act.[62] Both Acts are recent and in part are a response to the inadequacy of municipal licensing in dealing with information problems. The Consumer Protection Act requires the registration of itinerant sellers, who are defined as 'sellers whose business includes soliciting, negotiating, or arranging for the signing by a buyer, at a place other than the seller's permanent place of business, of an executory contract for the sales of goods or services.' The Act's provisions for registration are in fact licensing provisions, since one cannot carry on business as an itinerant seller without being registered and registration is granted and revoked on the basis of expected financial responsibility in the conduct of business and on past conduct. The Act further provides for the investigation of complaints and for restraining orders.

The Consumer Protection Act in part is designed to deal with the same kinds of persons regulated under municipal licensing; that is, those persons who are more likely to abuse trusts and take advantage of information problems on the part of consumers. The Act can regulate businesses on a broader basis than can existing municipal licensing procedures; for example, it includes door-to-door salesmen or

61 R.S.O. 1980, c. 87
62 R.S.O. 1980, c. 55

driveway repairmen who are not covered under municipal regulation. In the context of this more general control, municipal licensing can be seen as providing an additional means of certification with respect to certain listed businesses over which there is municipal jurisdiction. It does not cover all businesses regulated under the Consumer Protection Act, nor does it, as we have seen, deal with the problem of financial capability except in certain cases to ensure the provider of services is insured.

The Consumer Protection Act provides remedies to information problems that go beyond those provided by municipal licensing. The Act provides for the recission of executory contracts by the consumer within two days of signing such contracts and prohibits misleading advertising. It thus enables consumers to seek out and discover more information and reconsider their decision to purchase goods and services. It also provides more information by requiring disclosure (where applicable) of the cost of borrowing. (Municipal licensing does, however, cover some businesses that the Act does not deal with because parties may not have entered into an executory contract.) Municipal licensing may serve as a means by which to increase the costs of violations of the Consumer Protection Act if the latter is considered in evaluating applications for licence renewal. In this way it can be seen as a supplement to the Consumer Protection Act, even though it is a much narrower form of regulation.

The Business Practices Act is another provincial statute that seeks to deal with the information problem in the marketplace. It prohibits false, misleading, or deceptive consumer representations and provides for recission and exemplary damages for breach of the statute. As well, there is provision for the director, who has wide powers of investigation, to make certain orders to individuals in order to protect consumers and stop unfair practices. This Act, like the Consumer Protection Act, is much wider in scope than municipal licensing authority. It is not limited to certain businesses; it deals directly with the problem of false information. Municipal licensing again can only be seen as a supplement to such legislation.

Municipal licensing can be a cost-effective means of supplementing provincial legislation. Indeed, where local licensing authorities use their powers to facilitate settlements of consumer complaints (as is done in Metropolitan Toronto), they provide a means by which consumers can seek redress without having to resort to the courts. Moreover, such local authorities may serve as an additional means by which consumers can be informed of protection afforded by provincial legislation. This potential role of municipal licensing authorities as both arbitrators and sources of information to consumers is one which could well be expanded. In effect, the existence of municipal licensing authorities provides an additional potential channel for information and informal adjudication which supplements both the role of direct provincial regulation and also the role of private consumer information agencies.

4 Other provincial regulation

Besides the two Acts discussed above, there are a number of specific areas where municipal licensing supplements provincial legislation. While in some cases the overlaps are obviously unnecessary (reflecting vestigial municipal regulation now supplanted by provincial regulation), most of them are intentional.

A number of overlaps exist in licensing highway transportation. The Municipality of Metropolitan Toronto runs an ambulance service under the authority of the Municipality of Metropolitan Toronto Act[63] and is given authority to set exams and regulate communications. Ambulances are also more generally regulated under the Ambulance Act.[64] Automobile wreckers are licensed under both the Highway Traffic Act and under the Municipal Act.[65]

Intermunicipal public commercial vehicles and drivers are regulated by the provincial government under the Public Vehicles Act and the Public Commercial Vehicles Act,[66] while those public vehicles operating solely within a municipality are regulated generally at the municipal level with limited provincial involvement under the Highway Traffic Act. Supplementary municipal regulation for taxi drivers is appropriate, it is suggested, because of the need to ensure that they have a knowledge of local geography.

There are a number of overlaps in the licensing of trades. Under Section 10(1) of the Apprenticeship and Tradesmen's Qualification Act, the Lieutenant Governor in Council may designate any trade as a certified trade and may provide for separate branches within the trade. Once a trade has been certified, no person other than an apprentice can work in it unless he holds a subsisting certificate. The Act also provides for regulations regarding the length of time of apprenticeships and for the passing of exams. As mentioned earlier, the municipality of Metropolitan Toronto also regulates with respect to competency in certain trades. In the case of plumbers and electricians, there is a supplementing of provincial certification to ensure, it is suggested, the sophistication required for that particular municipality, while in the case of barbers and driving school instructors (the latter being licensed under the Highway Traffic Act) provincial regulation is sufficient for a municipal licence.

A seemingly vestigial overlap is evident in the area of fuel dealers: the Energy

---

63 R.S.O. 1980, c. 314 s. 189 (2)
64 Ibid., c. 20
65 Ibid., c. 198 s. 41(1) and 302 s. 228 respectively
66 Ibid., c. 425 and c. 407 respectively

Act[67] provides for provincial licensing of hydrocarbon appliance installers (furnace installers) and contractors and for the licensing of hydrocarbon handlers. For handlers, the Energy Act further provides that it overrides any municipal bylaw. Metropolitan Toronto, through its bylaw, although it has authority to regulate fuel dealers, licenses and regulates in a much more limited way and directs its regulation to the quality, the weighing, and the delivery of coal. The municipalities are therefore left with an area of regulation in this field that, although it may be seen as supplementary, is not really needed today and is redundant.

Some overlaps reflect local regulation of negative local externalities and provincial regulation for very different purposes. For example, milk distributors, milk plant operators, and milk plants are regulated under the Milk Act,[68] while municipalities are left to supplement this regulation by licensing milk vendors, presumably as an adjunct to their regulation as local retail businesses. Service stations are regulated at both the provincial and municipal levels. Under the Gasoline Handling Act[69] a licence is required for the commercial handling of gasoline to ensure safety. Municipal regulation appears to supplement such regulation by preventing undue minor externalities, such as the parking and storage of cars or the removal of snow onto sidewalks. Meat inspection is another area of shared jurisdiction between the province and local municipalities. The province under the Meat Inspection Act (Ontario)[70] deals with the slaughtering of meat in plants; municipalities can supplement provincial regulation by licensing retailers to also ensure its wholesomeness. Tobacconists are also regulated in a similar way; wholesale sellers are licensed provincially under the Tobacco Tax Act, and retailers are licensed municipally under the Municipal Act.[71] Trailers are licensed at both levels of government. The province, under the Highway Traffic Act, Section 7(2)(b), seeks to deal with them as vehicles on the highway, while municipalities license them once they are parked in trailer camps, presumably differentiating between externalities as a result of location within the municipality and on the road. Both the province, under the Tourism Act[72] and the Innkeepers Act,[73] and the municipalities, under the Municipal Act, may regulate tourist camps and motels. In this case provincial regulation is directed towards information problems in terms of the provision of services honestly and for value, while municipal regulation deals with externalities because of location.

---

67 Ibid., c. 139 s. 12–14
68 Ibid., c. 266
69 Ibid., c. 185 s. 6
70 Ibid., c. 260
71 Ibid., c. 502 s. 3 and c. 302 s. 231 (2) respectively
72 Ibid., c. 507
73 Ibid., c. 217

Pawnbrokers are also regulated both provincially and locally. Recent amendments to the Municipal Act enable municipalities to regulate the clothing worn by persons working in eating and drinking establishments. That amendment, and the bylaw passed under it, supplements the detailed regulation and licensing of drinking establishments already found in the Liquor Licence Act.[74]

Municipal licensing can be seen as a useful supplement to provincial licensing. That supplement, however, is a patchwork with varying reasons or rationale. In some cases municipal licensing appears redundant. In other cases it can be seen as an adjunct of provincial regulation. In the latter cases, the overlap between provincial and municipal regulation could be made more rational through better utilization by the province of the opportunities for more effective local implementation provided by the existence of municipal licensing authorities.

5 The effectiveness of municipal licensing

It has been suggested that municipal licensing has no clear purpose, that it serves a number of different ends with respect to many different businesses. It seeks to deal with informational problems, with externalities, with competency, quality and quantity of goods and services, with public morality and general market regulation. Finally, it supplements other legislation. In some situations, it serves more than one of these functions.

One of the main reasons advanced for the use of licensing is that it is flexible and a sensitive legal tool. It can, for example, overcome the limitations of the criminal law, described earlier, and it can be applied, case by case, more easily than general legislation. Yet municipal licensing does not appear to be very effective when viewed in totality, except as an adjunct to provincial regulation. It is a useful device to respond quickly to issues as they arise, since the legislative process at the municipal level is quicker than at the senior levels of government. It is also useful in serving, in a very minimal way, the goals discussed earlier at a rather low cost to the community. However, it is not a sophisticated independent regulatory scheme with its own integrated rationale. Nor can it at present successfully fulfill the purposes it seeks to achieve.

The Municipality of Metropolitan Toronto indicates in an internal study that fourteen out of forty-seven businesses examined should no longer be regulated under the bylaw.[75] The reason for this is that regulation of many of the businesses is an anachronism. A further reason is that in all fourteen of the businesses suggested for deregulation there is no active enforcement. Moreover, the Metro-

---

74 Ibid., c. 244
75 *Review of the Licensing Function in Metropolitan Toronto*, November 1977, p. 36–44. This figure of fourteen is our determination.

politan Licensing Commission can be seen as dividing its work into two general categories. One category includes businesses with respect to which the commission has enacted detailed regulations. Activities in this category include taxis, cartage firms, driving school instructors, school bus drivers, tradesmen (including plumbers, electricians, heating installers, building renovators, and drain installers), and places of amusement (including adult entertainment parlours and body rub parlours). The other category includes the rest of the businesses licensed by the commission. With respect to this latter category there are generally no detailed provisions or active regulations by the commission. The regulation of milk stores, bread stores, shoe repair shops, tobacconists, circuses, and barbers takes virtually none of the commission's time in hearings and involves merely the formality of issuing a licence. Moreover, of the thirty-three activities in which continued licensing was recommended, only sixteen were subject to active enforcement by the commission staff.[76] In the case of those businesses not subject to active enforcement, the effect of municipal licensing is limited to providing a registry of businesses and further providing an institution for dealing with consumer complaints.[77]

The businesses which are more actively regulated by the commission appear to be those where public concern is high with respect to one or more of the purposes suggested above. The trades businesses are actively regulated, and there are substantial information problems with respect to them because they do not provide their services in a fixed location and because customers must rely on tradesmen for their information. Adult entertainment parlours are actively controlled because of public concern regarding morality and externalities, while taxis are actively regulated because of both industry pressure and public complaints. It should be noted as well that fire, building, and public health standards do not involve the commission in enforcement through its staff. Rather, complaints are made to the commission which may then revoke a licence.

Enforcement of the licensing bylaw by the commission is done in two ways. One is the use of prelicensing screening and testing. The other is by dealing with complaints. The screening of persons with respect to driving and criminal records is used particularly for cabs, cartage, trades, and adult entertainment businesses. In the area of cab licences, however, only 1–2 per cent of the 10,000 applications received annually are actually considered by the commission because of criminal and driving records. Most cab licences are issued without a hearing. In addition, in the taxi business the commission regularly checks the meters of cabs and the

---

76 Ibid.
77 As noted in Section IV(b), it is also possible that some of the activities not closely regulated were instances of 'placebo' regulation.

interior condition of cabs at predefined times twice a year.[78] Once again, this can only be seen as relatively crude regulation, because both the meter and the interior can be temporarily improved by the operator before the inspection. The posting of the name and number of the commission in the cab so that cab customers can call the commission with complaints has not resulted in numerous complaints, but the potential for complaint has an obvious deterrent value and is more likely to be effective than the prearranged inspections.

The regulation of the taxi and cartage business can thus be seen as providing some protection for the public from informational problems. It would appear safe to conclude that the licensing provisions provide a relatively unsophisticated screening process where there is no economic return to the employer for providing such a process, and that they further provide some general and specific deterrence. A similar conclusion can be reached with respect to the similar provisions for cartage drivers. The screening provisions for school bus drivers, driving school instructors, and adult entertainment operators and employees can be seen in the same light.

The requirement of a licence is not uniformly enforced. In order to operate cabs or cartage trucks with a firm's name on it, a licence must also be displayed, and this is relatively easy to enforce by external examination. Furthermore, in these businesses there is a vested interest on the part of operators to ensure that all persons carrying on the business are licensed and governed by the same rules. Therefore, although bandit cabs do operate in Metropolitan Toronto, they are often reported by drivers licensed by the commission. They are easily identified and concentrated in the downtown area.

With respect to the trades, enforcement is more difficult, and the usefulness of licensing is perhaps less obvious. Services can be provided by persons operating in unmarked vehicles who do not advertise their services; the provision of the service is so scattered that the requirements of a licence are virtually impossible to enforce.[79] The commission therefore will often only hear of breaches of requirement for a licence after a customer reports dissatisfaction with the services received. This, of course, defeats one of the main purposes of licensing, which is to operate prospectively. The commission, moreover, has no set policy to ensure that all tradesmen are licensed. In certain trades this is not a serious problem, because in plumbing, electrical, and certain construction jobs there must be inspection by municipal inspectors under the Ontario Building Code or other

78 Metropolitan Toronto Police Force: Investigation of Metropolitan Toronto Licensing Commission, February 1978

79 What this implies is that there are in effect two markets for tradesmen's services: one in which producers advertise through public phone listings, signs on trucks or at job sites, etc.; the other consisting of producers who operate in a less public fashion.

legislation, and this may result in notifications of breach of the licensing bylaw. The problem, of course, is that those who are not licensed may not have their work inspected. Plumbing, electrical, and contracting work can be done by an un-licensed tradesman who does not inform his customer of requirements for inspec-tion. The licensing requirements therefore can be seen as primarily aimed at tradesmen who are licensed as masters and who advertise or otherwise conduct their business in a public manner. They are relatively ineffective in regulating fringe businesses.

Attempts to control competency, quality, and quantity standards through muni-cipal licensing by pretesting make only a minor contribution to protection from externalities and informational problems. In part, this is because general proficiency standards are already required in the important trades at the provincial level. Beyond this, the use of municipal testing ensures a general level of com-petency on the part of the supplier but not on a particular job for a client. As a result, the building trades are subject to inspection on a job-by-job basis in many situations at the municipal level.[80] The commission in fact relies on this testing to ensure that competency, quality, and quantity standards are met. The argument that more sophisticated municipalities require greater competency because of more sophisticated construction techniques and buildings is weak. Complex buildings imply sophisticated clients supervising construction, so that information problems are less severe.[81] In addition, under the Building Code most buildings of any consequence must be inspected, and any concerns regarding externalities can be dealt with in that way.[82] Once again, it would appear that municipal licensing is not serving an important role in reducing externalities or information problems through testing.

Municipal licensing can provide enforcement by investigation of complaints. The Metropolitan Toronto Licensing Commission in 1978 investigated 852 com-plaints with respect to its 8222 trade licences. According to the commission's view, all but thirty-two of these were resolved. By resolved, however, it is meant

---

80 This is required under the provisions of the Building Code Act.
81 See Dewees, Makuch, and Waterhouse, 'An analysis of the practice of architecture and engineer-ing in Ontario,' Working Paper no. 1, prepared for the Professional Organizations Committee (1978).
82 S. 3.1.1 of the Ontario Building Code 0. 1980 R.R.O. 87 provides that all buildings used for public assembly for institutional purposes and high-hazard industrial occupancies must be in-spected, and that all buildings over a certain size used for residential, business or mercantile purposes or for medium- or low-hazard industrial occupancies must be inspected and constructed in accordance with the Code. Furthermore, s. 2.3.1 requires plans to be prepared by an architect or engineer, and s. 2.4 states that the architect or engineer shall be responsible for the general review of the building during construction.

that: (a) the commission's inspector brought the customer and tradesman together, and an agreement satisfactory to both was worked out (this apparently happens in 80 per cent of the complaints); (b) there was no satisfactory agreement reached by the parties, and the inspector agreed that the customer was overcharged or received poor service and suggested a civil action at which the inspector would appear as an expert witness for the customer (the inspector can also recommend revocation of a licence if the bylaw has been breached); (c) the customer was told he had no reason to complain but that he could bring a civil action, and that the inspector if called as a witness would state this; (d) the commission had no jurisdiction.

The commission staff in this process appear to act as arbitrators with some authority to encourage settlements. This consumer ombudsman role is clearly useful. But the role of licensing powers in providing the moral authority for such arbitration is not a major one. Without a clear breach of the bylaw, revocation cannot occur. Moreover, revocation is not a meaningful preventive device without effective enforcement of the requirement for possession of a licence. A charge and conviction for breach of the licensing bylaw does not result in a remedy to an individual. The commission itself cannot, and does not, provide a remedy to the client. The transaction costs of going to court and the time and expense entailed are not lessened substantially by the licensing process. The commission does, however, play a role in reducing costs to the customer in a civil suit because its inspector can predict whether the client should bring such an action and provide expert testimony. It thus can be seen in dealing with the building trades that municipal licensing powers play a minor but useful role in helping the consumer who has suffered as a result of informational inadequacies. Licensing inspectors play a larger role by serving as informal arbitrators, and this informal function should be regarded as the principal benefit provided to consumers by current municipal licensing establishments.

The powers granted to permit the commission to limit the numbers of body rub parlours, adult entertainment parlours, and billiard halls were not accompanied by any substantial enhancement of the enforcement powers of the commisson. The Metropolitan Toronto bylaw sets a limit on the number of body rub parlours, but the actual number of licensed parlours is much lower than the limit.[83] The high entry fee and high standards in terms of cleanliness and screening of applicants might therefore appear more effective than authority to limit numbers. (Here the licensing system can be seen as being very successful, if success is determined by limiting the number of such facilities.) However, to the extent that such establishments were fronts for prostitution and other illegal activities, and licensing was an attempt at controlling such activity, it is doubtful that licensing has been successful

83 Supra, n. 75

in restricting immoral acts, though it may have reduced their visibility. Moreover, other regulatory tools were of greater importance in eliminating undesirable parlours.[84]

Under the provisions of Metropolitan Toronto bylaws, as was suggested earlier, many businesses technically have not been closely regulated. In fact, the collection of the fees and the issuing of a licence is the main activity of the commission with respect to such businesses. Although there are detailed regulations for such businesses as barber shops, hairdressers, and, recently, pet shops, these are not systematically enforced, apparently because the standards prescribed for such businesses are so detailed as to make enforcement impractical or so vague as to make enforcement impossible.

Provisions regarding barber shops, for example, require rolls of white paper on every chair, prohibit the use of steamed towels more than once without being laundered, and require the use of a fresh, clean band around the neck of every customers. Such provisions, though anachronistic are also unenforceable except with constant inspection and supervision.[85] More important, they do nothing to meet any of the purposes discussed above. There are no informational problems, externalities, morality, or market concerns that require such regulation. A person attending a barber shop can see and judge for himself the service he is receiving.

A similar example is that of pet shops. An amendment to the Metropolitan Toronto licensing bylaw regulating pet shops was passed in February 1979. Many of the provisions regarding feeding, clean water, size of cages, and so on are so detailed that a very large number of enforcement officers would be required to make the bylaw effective. Other regulations such as 'adequate' light and ventilation and prohibition of 'crowded' quarters and the sale of animals with 'obvious' signs of disease are so vague as to make the application of the bylaw difficult.[86] Moreover, as suggested earlier, such regulations serve no obvious purpose, especially since many are in fact in the self-interest of pet shop operators in any event. It may be argued that the regulations are in effect the result of attempts to legislate moral behaviour, in this case in response to concerns about ill-treatment of animals by owners of pet stores.

Although useless regulations that have arisen from the patchwork approach of licensing are clearest in businesses where there is no active enforcement, they are also found in areas where the commission does in fact attempt to regulate, for

---

84 Disorderly Homes Act, R.S.O. 1980 c. 120
85 There are of course different levels of enforcement. The fact that regulations are not systematically or uniformly enforced does not mean that they are ineffective; they may be utilized as the basis for revocation of a licence in response to complaints by consumers or other parties.
86 Bylaw No. 107-78, Schedule 22, as re-enacted by bylaw 58-79

example dress restrictions and codes of conduct for taxicab or cartage drivers or the refusal to allow school bus drivers to smoke cigarettes, tobacco or other substances while driving a school bus. The vagueness and unenforceability of such standards are clear. The major problem is, as in other areas of regulation, the persistence of regulation which has become anachronistic.

Success in accomplishing the goals of municipal licensing is not at all clear.[87] The system provides some service in terms of conciliation activities and expert witnesses and therefore may lower transaction costs with respect to the bringing of civil suits. It is not, however, generally used as an effective information agency for breaches of provincial legislation such as the Consumer Protection Act or the Business Practices Act. Yet the system provides a simple screening process that in certain businesses appears to be useful and a supplementary enforcement device for implementing other municipal regulations, though such enforcement could be more effectively obtained by giving municipalities improved direct enforcement powers. The overall result is one of sporadic success in achieving the goals of licensing.

Costs of Municipal Licensing
The non-comprehensive, makeshift nature and limited enforcement of licensing might at first sight suggest that the municipal licensing power would be best revoked. Yet municipal licensing is also beneficial, providing a rough screening process, aiding in the enforcement of other legislation and, most importantly, providing a useful process for conciliating disputes. It also implies costs.

An obvious element of cost is the direct administrative costs of regulation. The total revenue raised by municipal licensing in Metropolitan Toronto in 1977 was $2,042,178, and this was approximately $300,000 short of the cost to the municipality for carrying on the operations of the commission.

Other costs also arise from municipal licensing. The system, as has been indicated, is a relatively rough one, relying on a screening process based largely on criminal and driving records and a 'feel' for the applicant's character and his attitude towards his record. The refusal of a licence to an applicant means a state prohibition against his being able to undertake a particular occupation. To an individual, therefore, a refusal is costly and should only be justified on the clearest

---

87 In 1976 there were a total of 1903 convictions for breach of Metropolitan Toronto Licensing Bylaw 959 related to the taxicab business. Of this total there were 304 convictions for improper trip records; 95 convictions for no spare tires; 1 conviction for refusal of a fare; and 122 for having a dirty taxicab. The 944 non-taxi related convictions were spread over 38 licence categories. Of the total of 1903 convictions, 790 were related to the failure to have, post, or produce a licence.

of grounds. On the other hand, licensing is prospective, unsophisticated, and therefore subject to inaccuracies and arbitrary decision.[88] An important potential economic cost therefore is that of erroneous refusal to grant licences. Closely allied to this cost is the question of whether the informality of the process provides sufficient protection of individual rights.

Individuals bear the cost of the time to process applications and appear before the commission. It can be argued that these costs are not substantial as applicants are generally seeking approval for low-payment occupations and only about 1 per cent of all applications result in a hearing before the commission.[89] Attending a hearing usualy involves an afternoon of an applicant's time. The hearing itself is an informal process which in most cases takes only a few minutes. Approximately 90 per cent of applicants appear without a lawyer (legal aid cannot be received by a licensing applicant). In such cases there is questioning by the commission but no cross-examination. This lessens the monetary costs to individual applicants but may also lessen many of the procedural safeguards of a more formal process.

Another cost to be considered is the cost in income redistribution and losses of efficiency that result from interfering with the market and from restrictions on market entry. However, this cost, as suggested earlier, does not appear to be a major one. The very limited effectiveness of municipal licensing means that the income distribution effects are minimal. Rates and fees are generally not set at the municipal level, and restrictions on entry and requirements for carrying on business are generally ineffective and not actively enforced.[90] No evidence has been found of different rates being charged by licensed tradesmen and tradesmen without municipal licences. Nor is there evidence of serious restrictions on intermunicipal mobility of tradesmen, except with respect to taxicabs.

There have been examples of attempts by certain groups to increase or protect their incomes by local regulations. There has been lobbying in Metropolitan Toronto for the setting of cartage rates and for the regulation of tow-trucks. The impetus for the former arose from cartage firms concerned about low rates and

---

88 For example, one member of the Metropolitan Toronto Licensing Commission indicated that a person convicted of certain crimes viewed as particularly abhorrent to that commissioner would never be granted a licence regardless of the relevancy of the conviction to the carrying on of a particular occupation.

89 Appeals to the courts are taken in only five to ten applications a year.

90 The highest fee charged in Metropolitan Toronto is $3300 for the owner / operator of an adult entertainment parlour. The vast majority of fees are below $100. Major exceptions to this relate to taxicabs ($2500) and motorcycle racing ($1100). This has resulted in conflicts between drivers at Toronto International Airport who are licensed in Metropolitan Toronto and the City of Mississauga. There has been legislation to remedy the problem. The legislation allows cab drivers licensed in both jurisdictions to pick up passengers at the airport. There have also been concerns expressed about bandit cabs from other municipalities operating within Metropolitan Toronto.

increased competition coming from small firms. For the latter, the impetus arose in part to control the activities of certain individual tow-truck operators who used radios to obtain information about accidents and thus arrived at accident scenes before the tow-trucks of firms called by the police. There has thus far been no regulation of cartage fares, and although regulation of tow-trucks has been implemented, it does not deal with the problem of drivers obtaining information on their radios.[91]

Other examples of possible attempts to affect income redistribution can be seen in the regulation of hawkers and peddlers. Schedule 15 of bylaw 107-78 prohibits hawkers and peddlers who have carts from stopping for more than a certain time in any one location. It has been argued that the provision, although it can be seen as an attempt to prevent congestion on the streets, particularly in popular areas such as in front of the Eaton Centre in downtown Toronto, is also an attempt to prevent hawkers and peddlers from competing with regular stores in the municipality. There is no evidence that the provision has had any profound impact on competition or has resulted in a substantial redistribution of income to store owners.

The final area of municipal regulation which may affect income distribution is with respect to master plumbers, heating installers, and electricians, each of whom must first pass examinations under the Apprenticeship and Tradesmen's Qualification Act. The requirements of testing and licensing before a plumber, heating installer, or electrician can become a master suggest entry barriers and restrictions on intermunicipal mobility.[92] According to the Electrical Contractors Association of Ontario, the 'master' designation denotes a better understanding of the Ontario Safety Code and its application, because a journeyman licensed under the Apprenticeship and Tradesmen's Qualification Act may have only basic knowledge of the code and may have difficulty in calculating load requirements and estimating the cost of work. The Association also suggests that masters' licences ensure that electrical contractors have basic knowledge and skills in conducting a business. Masters should have a knowledge of workmen's compensation and unemployment insurance legislation, the Employment Standards Act,[93] and the Occupational Health and Safety Act,[94] as well as the municipal

91 Bylaw No. 107-78, Schedule 39 as enacted by bylaw 130-79
92 It should be noted that both the Technical Contractors Association of Ontario and the Mechanical Contractors Association of Ontario prefer province-wide standards with no restrictions on mobility within the province. Indeed, they encourage municipalities to include reciprocal provisions in their bylaws, and the Municipality of Metropolitan Toronto has reciprocity with five other municipalities.
93 R.S.O. 1980 c. 137
94 R.S.O. 1980 c. 321

bylaws regulating their trade.[95] This concern for the individual's competence in both the trade and the business reflects the Association's wish to protect the reputation of the industry generally and its desire to present to the public an image of a businessman who can be trusted.

The result of the requirement for a master's certificate is that over 50 per cent of applicants for certificates in the various fields failed to pass the master examinations in 1978,[96] with a resulting restriction on entry into those businesses. While it is impossible to determine the exact impact on income distribution, there was probably at least some effect and thus a cost to society and the individuals involved. The effect would be increased by provisions in the bylaw requiring all contractors to be masters or to employ masters and prohibiting masters from working for more than one contractor at a time.

Public benefits from these restrictions are difficult to see. Why ensure that electricians, plumbers, and heating installers are aware of legislation affecting the conduct of their business and not do so for others who carry on business within the municipality? Indeed, an individual's lack of general business expertise is not an appropriate reason to prevent him from carrying on a business. It does not fall within the purposes of municipal licensing suggested above. With respect to knowledge of safety requirements and protection from unsafe workmanship, it has been pointed out that codes are generally standardized, Ontario Hydro conducts on-site inspections (one of the requirements of the municipal bylaw as well), and on large projects the client would ensure that inexperienced electricians are not employed.

Income redistribution through regulations controlling the conduct of business activity or through restrictions on entry can be seen as a cost of municipal licensing. For society generally, it does not appear to be a substantial cost, and its major effects appear to be in the area of electrical work and plumbing. But the cost is borne by individuals and may be important to them, so that the lack of any tangible benefit to society[97] makes the costs less justifiable.

Finally, it should be noted that the mere choice of licensing as a regulatory mechanism has costs to the individual. Through the use of the municipal licensing process, certain freedom is lost and the ability of the state to interfere with individual liberty is enhanced. Indeed, by reversing the onus of the criminal law and placing it on the individual, by relying on a previous record to predict future

---

95 Brief of the Electrical Contractors Association of Ontario re: The Municipal Licensing Act 1978, Bill 105, dated 8 December 1978

96 Metropolitan Licensing Commission, Inter-Departmental Correspondence, 5 January 1979

97 It is interesting to note that the E.C.A.O. in its brief points out that about one-half of the province does not have municipal licensing of electrical masters. The Association can point to no evidence of any difference in safety records as a result of that lack of regulation.

activity, and by seeking to regulate on the basis of the 'character' of an applicant, municipal licensing results in greater interference with individual liberty than does the Criminal Code.

Conclusions

It is clear from the above analysis that municipal licensing in Metropolitan Toronto is not particularly effective on its own in fulfilling any of its purposes. The reasons for this failure do not arise from the internal administration of licensing in Metropolitan Toronto but rather are inherent in the current provincial conception of the role of licensing. The potential ways in which municipal licensing may best provide a useful regulatory tool do not seem to have been systematically evaluated.

Metropolitan Toronto has little ability to deal effectively with the purposes of licensing. There is no overall rational approach to its delegated regulatory powers in this area. The municipality is not granted jurisdiction over all trades or businesses, so it cannot deal with informational or externality problems in a comprehensive way. Although Bill 105 might seem to remedy this problem to a certain extent, it does so by allowing the Lieutenant-Governor in Council to designate by regulation a class or classes of business that municipalities cannot regulate; its primary effect is thus to transfer this designating power from the provincial legislature to the provincial cabinet. Moreover, even with wide jurisdiction over different types of business there is no comprehensive authority (either in current legislation or in Bill 105) for municipalities to deal in a substantive way with those businesses. There is no clear authority to deal with many aspects of informational problems and externalities because of overlaps in provincial and municipal jurisdiction. As a result, municipal licensing has been limited to relatively marginal functions.

Municipal licensing serves different functions at different times for different businesses, often responding in large part to relatively particular public concerns. It is makeshift, with no uniform rationale. In addition, it is administered at the municipal level by a commission that has no direct ties to the municipalities where much of the substantive municipal regulation occurs, i.e., zoning and planning, public health, and building inspection.

Municipal licensing cannot be seen to deal effectively with informational problems. It does provide a screening device to ensure that persons with relevant criminal records are not licensed to carry on a business and in this way serves to extend protection otherwise provided by criminal law. However, there is little evidence that the process is accurate, and there are significant process costs in denying access to work on the basis of inevitably arbitrary prospective judgments.

It cannot be seen to be dealing effectively with externalities. Licensing generally is not used to determine the appropriate locations of businesses, and if Bill 105 is adopted, this use of licensing will be specifically prohibited. The Public Health Act and the Planning Act are designed to deal directly with these matters and do so more comprehensively. Licensing is a supplement to them; it aids in the enforcement of bylaws passed under those two acts. It does not add substantial authority to municipal powers in this respect because licensing cannot be used as a replacement for zoning or public health regulations, and judicial decisions on this issue have put narrow bounds on licensing powers.

With respect to externalities and information problems that may arise from shoddy workmanship, as opposed to the creation of nuisances, municipal licensing provides no substantive protection. As we have seen, there is no clear authority to deal with civil liability through municipal licensing, so licensing cannot be used to allocate the the risks that materialize from such externalities. It attempts to regulate competency, quality, and quantity on a limited basis but is often too vague or too detailed to be enforceable. There is substantial regulation of building construction quality through inspection under the Ontario Building Code and substantive competency regulation under other provincial legislation. Perhaps the most useful competency regulation at the municipal level is the requirement that cab drivers attend the taxicab drivers' school, although even this requirement could be implemented through municipal certification and provincial licensing.

General market regulation is only possible in a few limited areas under existing legislation, notably the taxicab and cartage businesses. Even here, however, the municipality cannot regulate all aspects of the business. Moreover, given the fact that markets are often wider than municipal boundaries, there appears to be little reason to have general market regulation at the municipal level. If there is a rationale for regulating taxicab numbers and fares, such regulation would be better implemented at the provincial level so that it would be uniform within a market area.[98]

John Palmer's concluding remarks on the taxicab industry in this volume, suggesting that there is a case for regulating fares but not entry, is consistent with our approach, provided that the role of certifying a minimum level of competence and reliability is recognized. Our proposal would be to restrict the licensing authority to fare regulation and the establishment of minimum standards for driver knowledge and taxicab maintenance.

The regulation of certain aspects of public morality has, in recent years, been regarded as one of the more successful accomplishments of municipal licensing. It

98 The problem of fragmented municipal jurisdiction is particularly intense in the Toronto area and arises primarily because of the geographic limits of the so-called regional government (the Municipality of Metropolitan Toronto). Were Metro's boundaries coterminous with those of the economic region, Metro would be an appropriate jurisdiction to which to assign taxicab fare regulations.

should be noted, however, that the reduction in the number of such businesses as body rub parlours was accomplished at considerable process costs. Moreover, it can be argued that licensing may not even have been effective in limiting immoral activities, only in limiting their visible externalities.

In examining the use of municipal licensing in Metropolitan Toronto, therefore, it can be seen that municipal licensing is a patchwork cut from other regulatory schemes. It has no clear explicit or implicit rationale. In addition, it has process costs which cannot be ignored. It also has some costs in income distribution and market efficiency. Bill 105, which is to deal comprehensively with municipal licensing, does not substantially resolve these problems. Indeed, it may increase the likelihood that municipal licensing will be ineffective by restricting licence fees.

REFORMS

Impediments to municipal licensing
The nature and use of municipal licensing reflects, to a large extent, the legal status of municipalities. As delegates of provincial jurisdictions, municipalities need specific authorization for any power to be exercised. As a result, authority is delegated to municipalities piece-meal. Municipal jurisdiction with respect to licensing reflects that status and that method of delegating authority. It reflects, moreover, an approach on the part of the province to control municipal policy and to prevent the abuse of municipal power by the narrow and detailed delegation of authority.[99]

Because of their inferior legal status, municipalities are treated by the courts as inferior bodies. Even when a general power is delegated on occasion, it is narrowly construed or interpreted in such a way as to give it no effect. So too the power to license, regulate, and govern business has been narrowly construed by the courts, so that a patchwork of jurisdiction is applied to regulate the patchwork of eligible businesses.

Municipalities cannot choose to license businesses where informational problems or externalities are severe. They must have provincial authorization. Requests to license painters and outside contractors and sand-blasters have been ignored by the commission because the municipality has no authority to regulate such businesses. Lead plants, which caused great concern a number of years ago in

_____

99 For a detailed review of this problem with respect to other areas of municipal authority, see Jaffary and Makuch, *Local Decision-Making and Administration*, Royal Commission on Metropolitan Toronto, 1977. As is noted elsewhere, the narrow delegation of authority is an inefficient way of protecting against abuse; cf. Bossons, *Reforming Planning in Ontario*, chap. 4.

Toronto because of severe externalities, could not be dealt with under municipal licensing nor under any other municipal powers.

There can be no comprehensive rational attempt to deal with either the informational problems or externalities of local businesses through municipal licensing because regulation can only be undertaken on a business-by-business basis. As seen earlier, a number of licensed businesses such as barbers and boats for hire have no externality, informational, public, morality, or general market regulation problem that would justify the present licensing. It is understandable that bodies with such limited authority would be reluctant to forgo regulation in those areas where the authority exists, even if regulation is unnecessary or out of date.[100] Therefore, it can be argued that a legislative provision enabling Metropolitan Toronto to regulate a business is virtually a request to carry out that regulation because such power would not be granted unless such regulation were required. However, often the need for such regulation has not been analysed at the provincial level; the authority is granted because of political pressure with the expectation that municipalities will carefully consider the need for regulation since the legislation is permissive.[101] The purposes of municipal licensing are thus not clearly thought out at either level of government, and the consequence is a bias in favour of needless regulation.

While the method by which jurisdiction is granted to municipalities is a serious impediment to effective and useful municipal licensing, so is the more general approach of the courts to interpreting municipal authority and status. It is clear that because of provincial supremacy municipal bylaws cannot conflict with provincial legislation.[102] Where the province has seen fit to regulate in any way, it is difficult for a municipality to become involved. Even where there is no provincial or federal regulation, an attempt to regulate may be seen as interfering with the authority of the senior levels of government. As a result, the municipalities cannot deal with businesses in a comprehensive way. Moreover, they cannot even deal adequately with those businesses over which they do have jurisdiction. The substance of municipal bylaws is thus narrowly defined.

There are a number of examples of judicial decisions to this effect. The Metropolitan Toronto Licensing Commission could not refuse the licensing of parcel delivery vehicles on the ground that the applicant had been prohibited by a decision of the Foreign Investment Review Board from taking over another company. The Board had found that the takeover would not be in the best interests

100 Even though a 1977 Metro study proposed reducing or eliminating some anachronistic regulations, nothing has been done at the political level to implement these proposals.
101 The passing of legislation regarding body rub parlours is an example of this.
102 *Re Regional Municipality of Ottawa-Carleton and Township of Marlborough* (1974), 2. O.R. (2d) 297 (O.H.C.)

of the Canadian public, and the commission had equated this finding with its power to consider whether the carrying on of the business by the applicant would be 'adverse to the public interest' under the bylaw. The court held that such a consideration was not a relevant one for a municipal licensing commission.[103] Although the court did not explain its reasons in detail, this case reflects the view that municipal licensing must be limited in scope. As a result of this approach, it has been held that municipalities cannot, without specific authorization, require a deposit of funds with the licensing authority as proof of financial responsibility. In addition, an attempt by the Metropolitan Toronto Licensing Commission to prevent cab drivers from being required to pay into an accident claim fund run by the owners of cabs was also struck down by the courts. In the latter case, the municipality was seeking to prevent owners from shifting the costs of all accidents to cab drivers. The court held that this provision of the bylaws was invalid because its sole purpose was to regulate the financial relations between owners and drivers, and this was not provided for in the enabling legislation.[104]

These decisions indicate that municipalities cannot, without a clearer granting of authority, regulate all aspects of a business. The courts have not clearly indicated what is beyond municipal jurisdiction, but any licensing bylaw must take into account that regulation is to be for municipal purposes and thus generally should not relate to matters of provincial or federal concern unless specifically provided for in the legislation.

For this reason special provision has been made for hours of operation and numbers of businesses in the legislation. Municipalities cannot regulate with respect to these substantive issues without such provision. It is difficult to expect municipal licensing to function in a meaningful way in a legal environment where it cannot deal with all aspects of a problem. For example, for informational problems, disclosure requirements and certain contractual rights are an important substantive way of dealing with the problem. A municipality probably could not enact such requirements without special provincial legislation. Externalities may be best solved by regulation regarding contractual warranties and the posting of notices regarding warranties. Once again, municipalities have no authority to implement such provisions as part of a comprehensive scheme of licensing, and such protections are in any case better accomplished through provincial regulation. Similar concerns can be raised with respect to general market regulations, as the earlier example of prohibiting payment into an accident claim fund suggests.

In addition, municipalities cannot easily use licensing to supplement other regulatory devices or to create as finely tuned a regulatory device as would be

---

103 *U.P.S. Ltd. v. Metro Licensing Commission*, 2 M.P.L.R. 169 (Ont. Div. Ct.)
104 *Re Christie Taxi Ltd. and Doran* (1975), 10 O.R. (2d) 313 (O.C.A.)

possible. For example, municipal licensing cannot be used as a substitute to zoning, although both are municipal powers. The Licensing Commission therefore does not reject licensing for businesses on the grounds of location only and generally, without specific authority, does not regulate with respect to location.[105] Licensing bylaws, moreover, cannot create subcategories of business as defined in the bylaw and regulate such categories differently.[106] Municipal licensing might be more effective in dealing with informational problems, however, if classes of high-risk licences were established. It would seem unlikely that such categories could be established under the present legislation. Businesses cannot be classified according to size, location, or sophistication of employees.

With these limitations on municipal licensing it is perhaps surprising that municipal licensing succeeds in accomplishing anything at all. It is a legal device with restrictions that arise from the nineteenth century, and it is not able to use more sophisticated and comprehensive approaches to regulation that are found today. Not surprisingly, therefore, the licensing commission relies heavily on police records, and its best recent success has been in acting as a supplement to the Criminal Code in reducing the number of body rub parlours. In these two areas it is closely allied to the Criminal Code, a legal tool that is relatively simple in application because it merely prohibits certain conduct.

In summary, the legislation does not provide municipalities with an ability to deal comprehensively with informational problems arising from business activity. The language of the legislation is not broad enough to allow for bylaws to be passed for the protection of consumers through regulating contractual relationships. Similarly, with respect to externalities and market regulation, there is nothing in the legislation that would permit a general, comprehensive and finely tuned approach to licensing. It is in part for this reason that other legislation has grown up at the provincial level to deal with consumer protection in a more general way. The desirability of uniform regulation within the province with respect to civil and contractual rights is clearly also a consideration.

The limited nature of municipal jurisdiction is not in itself undesirable; there are a number of advantages to the present dual jurisdiction, with its overlapping municipal and provincial regulation. However, there is potential for improvement in regulating efficiency through a better definition of the role and purpose of municipal licensing as a supplement to provincial controls.

The proposed Municipal Licensing Act, Bill 105

The Municipal Licensing Act, 1982, removes from the Municipal Act a large number of provisions for the licensing and regulating of a variety of specific trades

---

105 *R. v. Donald B. Allen Ltd.* (1975) 11 o.r. (2d) 271. 65 d.l.r. (3rd) 599 (Div. Ct.)
106 Disorderly Homes Act, r.s.o. 1980 C.120 and *Re Bunce and Town of Cobourg*, [1963] 2 o.r. 344 (o.c.a.)

and businesses and confers general authority on all local municipalities to pass bylaws to license, regulate, and govern any business carried on within the municipality, providing the terms of any such licensing or regulating bylaws do not conflict with provincial statutes or regulations dealing with any particular business.

The Act can be seen, therefore, as attempting to deal with municipal licensing in a comprehensive way. It does so by removing the power to license specific businesses or trades and redefines business in a general way to mean 'any trade, calling, business, occupation, manufacture, or industry and includes the sale or hire of goods or services on an intermittent or one time basis.' The Act therefore deals in part with the patchwork problem descibed earlier by providing wide jurisdiction over all types of businesses. This would eliminate the problem of municipalities being unable to deal with certain businesses because they are not listed in provincial legislation.[107]

However, the Act provides that where there is conflict with any provincial regulation the provincial regulation will prevail. This legislative restatement of case law may well reintroduce the problem of limited municipal jurisdiction because the courts may define conflict very broadly and restrict municipal authority accordingly. Furthermore, the legislation does not deal with the patchwork of *purposes* for municipal licensing or the patchwork of substantive *jurisdiction* for municipal licensing. The Act uses the words currently found in the Municipal Act – 'licensing, regulating, and governing' – and does not give any clear indication of the breadth or purpose of the authority granted under that section. The Act does state that the power to license, regulate and govern includes:

1) the power to prohibit the carrying on of a business without a licence;
2) the power to license individuals;
3) the power to regulate hours;
4) with certain exceptions, the power to require competency exminations and to exempt applicants from such exams;
5) the power to regulate, govern, and inspect premises, facilities, equipment, vehicles, and other personal property;
6) the power to require persons carrying on business to maintain adequate insurance;
7) the power to refuse, revoke, or suspend a licence.

All these powers are now exercised by municipalities under the existing provisions of the Municipal Act. To a large extent, therefore, the Municipal Licensing Act gives legislative sanction to the present patchwork of municipal licensing that has arisen without a clear rationale. It is a crystallization in legislative form of the

---

107 It should be noted, however, that under the Bill, the Lieutenant-Governor in Council can exempt businesses from municipal regulation.

present situation. The problem of attempting to regulate all facets of a business in a comprehensive way is not solved; indeed, by specifying the powers included in the authority to license, the new legislation may well limit the municipalities to those powers and exclude broader powers such as the power to regulate contractual relationships or the narrower power to require the posting of bonds.

Where the Act does alter the status quo, the change is minor and sometimes restrictive. It enables municipalities to establish a class or classes of businesses and to separately license and regulate each class. This can provide municipalities with some increased flexibility, but there may well be litigation if any attempt is made in a licensing bylaw passed under the legislation to establish a 'sub-class' or 'sub-classes.' A second change in the Act prohibits municipalities from requiring a competency test when an individual has a certificate of apprenticeship or qualification issued under the Apprenticeship and Tradesmen's Qualification Act. The Municipal Licensing Act therefore reduces overlaps between municipal and provincial regulation in the area of plumbers and electricians. The Act prohibits the refusal of a licence on locational grounds alone, while the present legislation merely provides a 'non-conforming use' for businesses already in a location. This provision also prohibits the issuing of a licence for a proposed business where the location of the business would be in contravention of any planning legislation. These provisions are a reflection of present case law and practice with respect to location and clearly limit any attempt to use licensing flexibly to deal with externalities and to supplement zoning.

The remaining provisions of the Municipal Licensing Act provide for the special authority over body rub parlours, adult entertainment parlours, and billiard tables that is now found in the Municipal Act. They also provide for the repeal of a large number of specific provisions that would be unnecessary because of the general definition of business. Finally, the Act arbitrarily limits the amount to be charged for licences.[108] However, after pressure from municipalities and some interest groups, fees are now allowed so that administrative and enforcement costs can be recovered.

---

108 The provision of the Act with respect to fees has brought opposition from municipalities who fear that the cost of licensing would increase. Indeed, one of the rationales for the restriction was to discourage unnecessary licensing because it was felt that municipalities would not license activities as readily as when they could recover the costs of licensing. Interestingly enough, aside from municipalities, the main interest groups to speak in opposition were the Electrical Contractors Association of Ontario and the Mechanical Contractors Association of Ontario. This may well suggest that these groups benefit from municipal licensing. The Associations see municipal licensing with reciprocity as a stepping stone to meaningful regulation, that is, regulation at the provincial level, which has been rejected by the province in the past. (Interview with N.W. Purdy, Vice-President, e.c.a.o., 29 June 1978)

The Municipal Licensing Act is thus largely a codification of present municipal licensing practices and problems with the exception of the general definition of 'business.' It does not solve the many jurisdictional difficulties underlying the present municipal licensing system; it does not deal with the major issue of a rationale for municipal licensing; and in some cases, it may restrict what little flexibility is now found in the system.

Assessing the optimal degree of decentralization in regulation
This section discusses the level of government through which it is most useful to implement regulation, first for licensing to regulate product quality, then for licensing to control local externalities. In both cases the issue is a compromise between the flexibility attained by decentralized regulation and the advantages of province-wide uniformity. The costs of non-uniform regulation are increased barriers to mobility. The costs of centralized, uniform regulation are a reduced ability to tailor such regulation to meet local variations in perceived needs.

1 Quality maintenance regulation
The primary advantages of implementing regulation at the municipal level are twofold: first, the resulting decentralization of administration facilitates consumer use of licensing authorities as arbiters of contract disputes; second, the larger potential role for municipal politicians is likely to result in a greater responsiveness to consumer problems by the licensing administrators. Against these advantages must be set the possibility of abuse of discretionary powers by municipal politicians and the costs to producers of having to deal with non-uniform regulation in different municipalities.

It is useful to differentiate between entry regulation and continuing regulation. By entry regulation is meant the establishment of minimum competency standards for new entrants; by continuing regulation is meant the monitoring of product quality for ongoing producers. There are some advantages in establishing divided jurisdiction to deal with these different aspects of regulation. There are few obvious advantages in differing entry standards across the province to set against the advantages of facilitating producer mobility across municipal boundaries. Moreover, in the case of entry standards of tradesmen, competency standards established at the provincial level may more easily be reflected in provincially administered vocational training programs. The advantages of municipal regulation noted above apply primarily to ongoing business operations; there is consequently some advantage in having entry standards set by the province but licensing administered by municipalities. As is noted below, this division of responsibility is essentially current practice in Ontario.

Because of the potential for abuse of discretionary licensing power delegated to municipalities, it is necessary to provide for appeals from the exercise of this power. Under the present system, appeals from municipal decisions to reject or revoke licences are to the courts and thus are costly for small firms. It may be desirable to find ways of reducing appeal costs by providing for more informal appeal procedures.[109]

2 Externality regulation

In the case of externality regulation it is necessary to add to the two advantages of municipal-level regulation noted above a third advantage: the nature and cost of such externalities is likely to vary considerably from city to city as well as among localities within cities, so that there is a relatively high degree of local information required for correct specification of such regulation. It is useful for such regulation to be implemented at local level by officials and politicians responsive to local variations in regulatory needs. Such regulation, by virtue of dealing with externalities, should be closely integrated with local land-use regulation; this is another reason for implementing such regulation at the local level.

The need for local information in regulatory decisions is an obvious rationale for implementing regulation at the municipal level. Indeed, one of the principal ways in which the potential usefulness of municipal licensing can be expanded is to use it as a means of implementing concerns over negative local externalities potentially associated with particular land uses and so permitting a more efficient form of land-use control than the present reliance on exclusionary zoning. Other areas in which a need for local information is evident include situations in which it may be desirable to ensure that tradesmen (e.g. capenters or plumbers) have a working knowledge of municipal regulations that supplement provincial standards. While the importance of municipally varying building standards has been reduced in the building trades by the adoption of provincial and federal (CMHC) building codes, situations remain in which municipal licensing is still a means of facilitating the enforcement of such municipal requirements.[110]

3 Other factors

In a number of situations the existence of local administrative institutions to implement regulations for which local knowledge is required provides a convenient, low-cost means of implementing other regulations which could be poten-

---

109 In the case of municipal decisions on land-use controls, appeals from such decisions may be heard by the Ontario Municipal Board, a quasi-judicial review body established by the province.
110 It may of course be argued that such standards could be enforced directly through municipal inspection and approval of building permits. Nevertheless, as noted earlier, the licensing authority provides a supplement to direct enforcement that can reduce the overall private and public cost of regulation.

tially administered at any level of government. Once it is necessary to set up a licensing authority for some purposes at the local level, the marginal cost of using this authority for the implementation of some other regulatory functions may be relatively low. Moreover, use of a local institution has the obvious advantage of providing a decentralized means of administering regulations with high local accessibility. For these two reasons, the implementation of provincial consumer protection legislation may potentially be made more effective by utilizing municipal licensing authorities as a supplementary means of enforcement and also as a supplementary channel through which consumers may seek informal means of redress.

The use of municipal licensing authorities as a means through which to implement certain provincial regulations more cheaply is of particular relevance in situations where local businesses are being licensed municipally for other reasons. For example, where a business is being licensed and inspected to control negative local externalities, it may be cost-effective to combine the examination with inspection for other purposes. The primary determinant of the attractiveness of combining the two types of inspection will be the consistency of the information and training requirements for each inspection.

The foregoing comments are directed primarily at defining the circumstances under which local rather than provincial implementation of regulation is appropriate. It should be noted that they also have implications for where such regulatory functions should be located in a two-tier municipality. Where a two-tier municipality is large (such as in Metropolitan Toronto), there is a strong case for distinguishing between licensing powers that should be implemented by the upper-tier municipality and licensing that should be done by the local (lower-tier) municipality. Licensing functions that are particularly related to the control of negative local externalities should be integrated with the use of zoning powers and thus assigned to local (lower-tier) municipalities.[111]

In general (with some exceptions) most of the municipal regulation of trades and businesses currently implemented through municipal licensing overlaps provincial regulation and would be better integrated with the latter. Where municipal regulation does not overlap directly, it may have an income distribution effect. The current assortment of municipal business licensing powers are in part a survival of early attempts at consumer protection that have been largely supplanted by subsequent provincial regulation in the form of the Consumer Protection Act and the Business Practices Act. As such, there is at best a very marginal return to maintaining an ineffective duplicate set of regulations at the municipal level.

111 Reasons for assigning detailed land-use controls to lower-tier municipalities are discussed in Bossons, *Reforming Planning in Ontario*, section 7.2.

Where municipal intervention clearly has a rationale is in the regulation of businesses where the certification of locality-specific knowledge is important (as in certification of taxi drivers' knowledge of local roads) or where local information is required in order to administer regulation more effectively. The regulation of employment standards or the certification of tradesmen's skills is clearly not an area in which locality-specific knowledge is very relevant. Accordingly, our principal conclusion is that municipal establishment of business regulation standards should be limited to those areas where local knowledge is important, and that the existing powers to duplicate provincial regulation of consumer protection should be curtailed. Contractual relationships should be governed on a uniform basis across the province, and municipal regulation should not result in locally-varying standards.

This does not imply that current municipal licensing bodies cannot play a useful role in assisting consumers in dealing with tradesmen in situations where information about competence and reliability are difficult to obtain. However, such a role should be limited to information dissemination. To go beyond this to regulate entry for the purpose of protecting consumers is to intervene in a function that is better done in a uniform manner by the province and so integrated with other provincial regulation that is applicable to the same firms.

Where municipal licensing seems to have been most useful in the consumer protection area is in its contribution to the resolution of disputes between tradesmen and consumers. This is a valuable function, and it should be expanded. As has been noted, the effectiveness of a licensing inspector as an arbiter in such disputes is often not so much dependent on potential revocation of the municipal licence as on his ability to testify as an expert witness in civil suits.

In the consumer protection area, municipal licensing can play a useful administrative function. There are advantages to decentralized administration of provincial regulation of trades, and such decentralization can be effectively achieved utilizing municipal licensing bodies for this purpose. However, the regulatory role of municipal licensing should be confined to the registration of businesses and certification of provincially defined standards. Accordingly, the focus of municipal licensing activities should be more clearly oriented to serving a consumer ombudsman function in which the primary emphasis of licensing administration is in supplementing provincial regulation and providing for the evaluation and, where possible, resolution of consumer complaints.

New directions for municipal licensing
The most telling criticism of the present municipal licensing system is that it is not really directed at municipal problems. That this should be so is perhaps a reflection of the fact that the purpose and function of municipal licensing has never been

systematically examined, and that the present system of municipal licensing is largely a survival of nineteenth-century regulatory intervention that predates the introduction of broader provincial regulation.

Many of the present municipal powers to restrict entry into a business through licensing are neither effective nor necessary, and the exercise of entry regulation powers should generally be restricted to the provincial government. We propose that municipal powers to regulate trades and businesses should in general be limited to the certification of competence and reliability. Where it is necessary or useful for municipalities to go beyond this certification role to license entry, municipal powers should be limited to the establishment and enforcement of minimum standards. Resources now spent ineffectively in the attempt to enforce entry regulation for trades would, we believe, be better spent on advertising aimed at making consumers aware of the availability of information and arbitration services from municipal registration offices.

The major regulatory role of municipal licensing authorities should be in dealing with the externality problems which are of a local nature and should reflect the potential use of municipal licensing powers as a means of expanding municipal instruments for land-use regulation that deals with externality problems directly. Such problems arise from negative local externalities that may be associated with particular land uses.

At present, local externalities of this type are now dealt with only through the powers granted to municipalities by the Planning Act. Although such power has recently been expanded to include more detailed development control over new buildings, the focus of municipal planning regulation is on the use of land as may be categorized in advance. That regulation does not include the ability to set performance standards in the conduct of the business on a case-by-case or business-by-business basis. For example, municipalities can enact zoning bylaws to specify whether restaurants shall be allowed in a certain area, but cannot set in those bylaws regulations on hours of operation or control the number of people who can be served in order to prevent parking problems or the disposal of garbage by the restaurant. Those matters are externalities which can be dealt with by zoning bylaws only through forbidding restaurants entirely. Similarly, municipalities can zone with respect to whether land is used for group homes and set certain standards respecting parking, building density, setbacks, height, etc. for those homes. They cannot deal with problems of the mix of people in the homes, the cooperation of the home with the surrounding community, or the noise emanating from the home, through the zoning bylaws technique. Providing for the licensing of land uses along with the control of them through zoning bylaws could enable municipalities to deal with the problems of externalities in a more comprehensive way and so permit municipalities to respond to neighbourhood demands for protection from potential negative externalities through instruments that are less draconian than simply forbidding the location of such uses in an area.

Such an approach would require removing the artificial distinction between licensing and zoning which is maintained in current legislative definitions of municipal powers. It would also require allocating such licensing powers to the municipal level actually concerned with local land-use regulation, namely the lower-tier or local municipality. While the regulation of trades and businesses should be either done at the provincial or regional (market-wide) level, the detailed regulation of local land uses should be implemented only at the local municipality level.

By permitting local municipalities to exercise powers to regulate the uses of land, an additional tool of land-use control would be made available to municipalities. The use of this tool should be subject to review by the Ontario Municipal Board in order to provide protections against the arbitrary exercise of municipal licensing power. In particular, it would be appropriate to provide that municipal exercise of licensing powers to regulate business activities should conform to criteria established by municipal bylaws that are subject to the same process of provincial review as zoning bylaws. This would be consistent with the proposed use of licensing powers as a form of performance zoning and would ensure that individual rights are subject to no less protection than would apply in the adoption by municipalities of zoning bylaws.

3
Municipal transportation regulation: cartage and taxicabs

JOHN PALMER

INTRODUCTION

The two major areas of urban transportation are the movement of goods and the movement of people. Often, when these movements involve a market transaction, i.e., are performed on a for-hire basis, they are regulated to some extent by the municipality. The cartage industry is the for-hire urban transportation-of-goods industry; the taxicab industry is the most important privately owned urban transportation-of-people industry. This study explores the rationales offered by municipalities for regulating these industries and studies the effects of the different regulations in various municipalities in Ontario and elsewhere.

The rationales offered for regulating municipal transportation are based almost entirely on arguments that unregulated competition would create inefficiencies and could seriously redistribute wealth away from disadvantaged groups. In more formal language, the arguments are based on market failure and equity considerations.

Market failure
The market failure rationale for regulation hinges on two types of market failure: the generation of externalities and the possible existence of economies of scale. The possible externalities most often mentioned by members of the urban transportation industries include congestion, noise, information, safety, and the threat of criminal activity.

Congestion and excessive noise can be caused as individual firms, each seeking to maximize profits, engage in a private calculus which ignores the imposition of costs on other economic units in society. This is a well-known problem for people residing in urban areas and has been discussed at length by urban and welfare economists. It has been argued by many people in the industries studied that regulation is necessary to deal with such problems. In the cartage industry, the problem most frequently arises as many firms attempt to make deliveries during the same period of the day to numerous stores and factories concentrated in one small geographic section of the municipality. Problems such as insufficient loading dock facilities and double parking add to the congestion and noise. In the taxicab industry, a prime example of the congestion problem arose in the Los Angeles area in the 1920s as taxicab drivers often literally fought over desirable waiting space in front of certain buildings. More recently, taxicab traffic at major airports has become an issue in many municipalities, and it often involves multi-level government negotiations concerning the appropriate regulations.

Information, or the lack of it, can be involved in market failure because obtaining information is not a costless procedure, and economies of scale in the collection and dissemination of information may make a more centralized activity more efficient socially. Information about rates, service reliability, and insurance available is of concern to consumers of the services of both the cartage and taxicab industries. It has often been suggested that regulation can reduce these information costs, both privately and socially.

Similarly, it has frequently been argued that minimum safety standards are required in these industries, not only to protect third parties but also to protect the consumers of the services. These arguments seem to take on more strength in the taxicab industries since the lives and physical health of third parties, including the people riding in the taxicabs, can be affected by the safety with which a taxicab is operated.

Criminal activity by itself is not an externality; it simply redistributes wealth from one economic unit to another. However the threat of criminal activity does create an externality in that economic units will use scarce resources to reduce the threat of such a redistribution away from themselves. It can be, and often has been, argued that regulations can be used to reduce the private and social costs arising from the threat of criminal activity in the cartage and taxicab industries.

Many of the externalities discussed above are claimed by some people to arise because of the nature of the technologies of the industries. Although the capital costs of entry are, relatively speaking, quite low, there is some feeling (perhaps akin to the Chamberlin excess capacity theorem in monopolistic competition) that firms in these industries are operating at rates of output for which marginal costs are less than the prices charged, and that they are in a constant scramble to cover their albeit low, overhead costs. This scramble, it is argued, gives rise to cut-throat competition in which safety and service reliability are sometimes sacrificed and consumers are given false information, even preyed upon by unscrupulous members of the industries. In municipalities in which licences to operate command high market prices, these overhead costs are not so low, but as will be argued later, the incentives are not much different.

On a firm basis, rather than on a vehicle basis, other types of economies of scale emerge. Large firms presumably have some advantages in operating dispatching services, negotiating exclusive-service contracts, and scheduling, and these advantages are apparent to some degree in both industries. If these economies of scale are important enough, they may give rise to monopolistic or tightly knit oligopolistic industries and justify some form of governmental intervention on natural monopoly grounds. The present study suggest that this possibility has considerably more merit in some taxicab industries than in any cartage industries.

Wealth redistribution
Regulations can be used to benefit three different groups: segments of the consuming population such as senior citizens; members of the industry who might benefit from safety regulations if they are employees or who might receive other benefits as either employees or employers; and potential entrants who need to be protected from their own misinformed fantasies by regulation.

Types of regulation
There are three categories of regulations in the municipal transportation industries. The first category consists of specific regulations designed to prohibit or require certain activities or standards of performance, such as driver safety, vehicle safety, driver knowledge of geography, and, in the Los Angeles taxicab industry, service promptness. The other two types of regulation are rate and entry regulations. These are often justified indirectly, as well as by arguments based strictly on rates, entry, and wealth distribution.

THE URBAN CARTAGE INDUSTRY

There are three broad reasons for regulating industries: natural monopolies,[1] consumer protection,[2] and cut-throat or chaotic competition. The latter is frequently used to justify regulation of the urban cartage industry.

Regulation of chaotic competition can take two general forms: price regulation and entry regulation. Price regulation is used in nearly all taxicab industries and some intercity trucking industries but in virtually no cartage industry. Entry regulation is used in most (but not all) taxicab industries and intercity trucking industries, but in only a few cartage industries. This study therefore examines entry regulations.

One basis for entry regulation in chaotically competitive industries is consumer

---

1 See, for example, any issue of the *Bell Journal*.
2 See, for example, S. Peltzman (1975), 'The effects of automobile safety regulation,' *Journal of Political Economy*, 677–725, and C. Stuart (1978), 'Consumer protection in markets with informationally weak buyers' (unpublished mimeo, University of Western Ontario).

protection. There may be some merit in regulations limiting entry to insured and bonded firms with safe drivers and safe vehicles. There are reasonable economic arguments to be made in favour of vehicle and driver safety regulations or in support of required basic insurance and financial bonding, but these arguments do not by themselves justify the requirement that potential entrants demonstrate to a regulatory agency that the public necessity and convenience will be enhanced by their services.

A second common justification for entry regulation is to reduce negative externalities. The argument in this case frequently (and fallaciously) assumes that the production process is such that negative externalities can be reduced only by reducing output in the industry.[3] Of course there are numerous alternative, and generally more efficient, methods of reducing negative externalities. If noise pollution is a concern, trucks can be required to install more effective mufflers; if air pollution is a concern, emission control devices can be required and inspected; and if congestion at rush hour is a concern, cartage firms can be required to pay more for supplementary licences which permit some of their trucks to be on the streets during rush hour. Numerous other, equally plausible, schemes abound. Thus broad-scale entry restriction is likely to be a very blunt, inefficient policy tool for dealing with specific problem areas.

A third major reason alleged for regulating entry into chaotically competitive industries is that the chaos of the marketplace tends to cause high volatility of prices and industry membership. This high volatility and instability is said to be a source of a major misallocation of resources as firms enter and exit the industry. With entry regulation, it is argued, fly-by-night operators will be excluded from the industry, and the municipality will have a stable industry to call on during peak and off-peak demand periods. Against this view, many economists emphasize the creative, innovative long-run effects of free entry and point to the efficiency of allowing mobile resources to satisfy peak demands.

A final ground for regulating entry is that potential entrants are generally uninformed about the volatility and uncertainty of the industry. They happen to see a potential for high immediate returns and falsely extrapolate these to high long-run returns. These potential entrants, it is said, need to be protected from themselves; stiff entry restrictions are really doing these people a favour. There are, of course, alternative solutions, such as requiring potential entrants to have some business training and some prior experience or knowledge of the industry. Furthermore, it is not clear that broad entry restrictions have much of an effect on this situation.

---

3 The classical theoretical model which reinforces this misconception is by J. Buchanan and C. Stubblebine (1962), 'Externality,' *Economica*, 371–84.

This study will briefly examine the validity of the third argument for entry regulation of the cartage industry: to stabilize industry membership.

Membership stability in the urban cartage industry: case studies

We begin with an examination of entry into and exit from the London, Ontario cartage industry from 1966 to 1976, where there was essentially free entry. Data for such a study were virtually non-existent. London once licensed firms in the cartage industry simply to keep information about them, but the City Clerk found that many firms entered the industry without bothering to get a licence, and the scheme was eventually dropped. The Yellow Pages of the London telephone directories for these years were used to determine entrants and exits from the industry. This procedure necessitated perusal of cartage, delivery, courier, and household moving listings to determine which firms were actually in the industry. In cases of doubt, the firms still in existence were called to determine the extent of their cartage activity. When a firm that had apparently left the industry could not be reached, the decision was based on the content of their advertisement in light of what was known about firms with similar advertisements. A firm was deemed to have exited from the industry if (1) it no longer appeared in the Yellow Pages, (2) it no longer appeared in the White Pages, (3) it had not simply changed its name. The latter criterion was tested by comparing telephone numbers and addresses from year to year. The study showed that entry and exit rates fluctuated considerably from year to year, but the total number of firms generally hovered near the average for the eleven-year period (this and all results are summarized in the accompanying Table). For comparison, a similar analysis was performed of the pizza restaurant and printing industries in London. These two industries were (somewhat arbitrarily) selected because, like cartage, they have low fixed costs and easy entry. Unfortunately for the research, both of these industries apparently experienced high growth rates until about 1973, after which they stabilized. Nevertheless, both the full 1966–76 period and the 1973–76 sub-period show that these industries were no more stable than the cartage industry in London. In other words, if industry stability is a desired goal, if the industry in London is judged to be unstable, and if entry regulation is proposed as the solution, all three industries (and probably more) deserve entry regulation equally on this ground.

By contrast, in Kitchener, Ontario, entry into the cartage industry is strictly regulated. Potential entrants must convince a regulatory board that some potential customers cannot get good service from incumbents in the industry and would be eager to use the services of the new firm. Because only firm entry, not truck entry, is regulated in Kitchener, existing firms forestall entry by enlarging their fleets.

A study of the Kitchener cartage industry was carried out in the same manner as for the London industries. The Kitchener cartage industry had considerably lower exit and entry rates than were observed in London. There was also a slight decline in the number of firms in the industry over the eleven-year period, though the total number was nearly constant over most of the period. It appears that, whether desirable or not, entry regulation in Kitchener has had an effect in stabilizing membership in its cartage industry.

One further aspect of entry regulation explored was its effect on new entrants: does entry regulation ensure that successful entrants have greater staying power than they would in unregulated markets? To answer this question, the number and percentage of entrants that exited during the year after entry in each of the industries were recorded. Although the Kitchener cartage industry had very few entrants leaving the industry during the first year after entry, the main reason was that the industry had very few entrants. The staying power of those who were allowed to enter that industry was not measurably increased, if at all, over the staying power of entrants in unregulated industries. It appears that entry restrictions, as imposed in the Kitchener cartage industry, had little, if any, effect on protecting potential entrants from themselves, especially in 1976.

London, with no entry regulations, and Kitchener, where entry is restricted, are the extremes. Similar analyses were conducted for Toronto, Thunder Bay, Windsor, Ottawa, and Sarnia. The cartage industries in each city had entry and exit rates marginally higher than those for the different industries in London (the highest exit rates were in cities where the number of firms was not growing over time), and the exit rates of new entrants were similar in all industries in all cities.

The results presented here suffer from all the difficulties inherent in small sample, case-type studies. But they strongly suggest that an unregulated cartage industry experiences no greater instability than is experienced in any other unregulated industry. Thus, cartage industries merit entry regulation on grounds of stability no more than do other industries. There also is some evidence (though based only on a small sample) that entry regulation may not increase the staying power of new entrants.

TAXICAB INDUSTRIES

Traditionally, economic studies of taxicab industries have been in-depth studies of one particular industry[4] or theoretical models of cruising industries with more

4 The most famous of these is by E.W. Kitch, M. Isaacson, and D. Kasper, 'The regulation of taxicabs in Chicago', *Journal of Law and Economics*, 14:2, Oct. 71. One of the first studies of this type was by R. Turvey, 'Some economic features of the London (England) cab trade,' *Economic Journal*, 79, 1961.

	London Cartage	London Pizza 1966–76	London Pizza 1973–76	London Printing 1966–76	London Printing 1973–76	Kitchener Cartage 1966–77	Toronto Cartage 1970–76	Thunder Bay Cartage 1966–78	Windsor Cartage 1967–77	Ottawa Cartage 1966–77	Sarnia Cartage 1966–77
1. Average no. of entrants	6.0	6.1	7.3	8.3	8.3	1.0	74.7	2.75	5.9	17.3	2.37
2. As a percentage of total	11.8	18.0	15.5	12.8	11.0	4.3	16.3	12.2	13.9	15.2	16.3
3. Average no. of exits	5.4	3.5	5	5.5	6.3	1.72	79.0	2.67	6.5	13.5	2.37
4. As a percentage of total	11.0	10.5	10.8	8.7	8.5	7.7	17.2	11.9	15.3	11.8	16.3
5. Average no. of entrants exiting after one year	2.0	1.9	3.7	1.9	3.0	0.3	31	1.0	2.3	5.22	0.9
(5) ÷ (1) as a percentage	33	31	51	23	36	30	41.6	36.3	39.0	30.3	34.6

general applicability.[5] Rarely have theoretical tools been used to analyse and tie together a discussion of several different taxicab markets, varying considerably in their structures and regulatory climates.[6] This study presents the results of interviews and other research from quite different municipalities.

Fare regulation

1 Rationale
Taxicabs are regulated in nearly every North American urban municipality. These regulations usually consist of fare and / or entry regulation. Fare regulation is often implemented for such reasons as consumer protection, the reduction of transaction, information, and negotiation costs, and the control of market power. The consumer protection rationale for fare regulation suggests that at the point at which a consumer wants a taxi, his elasticity of demand is very low, so that the first taxi to arrive would have an opportunity to extract a high fare if fares were unregulated. Opponents of this rationale point out that the first taxi may also have a highly inelastic short-run supply, so the customer may be able to extract a very low fare. It is clear that in each case, the actual fare will be determined by the relative bargaining strengths of the persons involved, which will depend in part on their relevant elasticities.[7] If there is any reason to believe that consumers will find themselves in poor bargaining positions, the consumer protection rationale for fare regulation may have some merit, especially if entry is regulated.[8]

Even if bargaining strengths are equal, bargaining takes time and involves

5 Among the better known of these studies are D. Orr, 'The "taxicab problem": a proposed solution,' *Journal of Political Economy* 77:1, Jan. / Feb. 1969, and A.S. DeVany, 'Capacity utilization under alternative regulatory constraints: an analysis of taxi markets,' Ibid. 83:1, Feb. 1975.

6 One possible exception to this statement is by M.E. Beesley, 'Regulation of taxis,' *Economic Journal* 83:329, March 1973.

7 For a discussion of these issues, see C. Shreiber, 'The economic reasons for price and entry regulation of taxicabs,' *Journal of Transport Economics and Policy* 9:3, September 1975; R.B. Coffman, 'Comment,' Ibid, 11.3, September 1977; and a rejoinder by Shreiber in the same issue.

8 The argument favouring fare regulation for consumer protection reasons is analogous to the legal doctrine of unconscionability under duress. See *The Port Caledonia and the Anna* [1903] 184, at 190, for a clear but perhaps extreme example of the doctrine. In this case, a tugmaster extracted a high fee for rescuing a ship in distress. An analogous situation in the taxi industry might arise for a passenger in a great hurry for some personal reason not related to the cost of providing him with taxi service. In the taxi, as well as the marine salvage, cases the problem may arise because the market for the specialized services offered is very thin: despite the expectation of receiving enormous revenues for the service, providers of the service are very reluctant to enter the specific, narrowly defined, industry since they cannot be certain when or where the services will be required. There seems to be a feeling among many people that the provision of such services

costs. Information concerning fares must be provided by taxis, their companies, or their dispatchers, and it must be obtained by customers. These costs need not be particularly high per taxi for larger fleets, which can spread the costs of advertising over many taxis, but they may be sufficiently high to cause substantially increased concentration, especially in some smaller markets. The reason for this increased concentration is that the advertising will generally cover the entire municipal area and not be directed at a specific customer at a specific moment.

Alternatively, each taxi could carry its own advertising by painting its fare structure on the side of the vehicle, as is done in New York City. The major difficulty with this alternative is that it would be quite difficult to paint an entire fare structure on the sides of taxis. Different runs of equal length involve different costs due to differences in the probabilities of securing additional runs or of being robbed, and it might be desirable to allow each taxi to determine these costs and set its fares accordingly. If the costs, and consequently the fares, do not vary much within a municipal area, each taxi may prefer to set standard fares, ignoring the small cost variations. Under these circumstances, allowing taxis to advertise fares on their vehicles may prove to be a working scheme. And it might even be desirable, under the consumer protection rationale, to *require* that the fares be painted on the vehicles, although competition would likely force nearly all taxis in such a market to follow suit if some taxis did so on their own.[9]

The third rationale for fare regulation stems from the desire to control market power. This rationale is not the same as the consumer protection rationale, which

---

involves no greater marginal costs than the provision of normal services, and that higher prices for such services would not and could not be high enough to attract entry into the provision of such special services. If this feeling is correct, the negotiated price will affect only the distribution of wealth between users and providers of the service; and if this is true, fare regulation may have some justification on equity grounds.

9 It must be remembered, however, that such a scheme would be practical only under two conditions: (1) that the cost structure not vary substantially between different trips and (2) that taxis be required to charge the advertised fares. While the first condition may be satisfied in such Ontario municipalities as London, Kitchener, Sarnia, or Windsor, which are fairly small cities and have a large amount of house and contract business compared to cruising business, the condition of equal cost structures is certainly violated in large metropolitan areas such as Toronto, Washington, and Los Angeles. As Kitch et al. point out ('The regulation of taxicabs in Chicago'), many areas of Chicago and New York City receive poor service at best because taxi drivers perceive that there are higher costs and / or risks involved with servicing such areas. Similar phenomena are seen in Los Angeles, Washington, and, on a much smaller scale, Toronto. The problem, of course, is that it is difficult for either a firm or a regulatory commission to formalize in sufficient detail the perceived costs and risks associated with serving different areas of a city and then to incorporate such differences into a city-wide structure, much less to fit such a detailed formalization of the fare structure on the side of a vehicle. Consequently, drivers tend to concentrate their efforts on the more profitable areas, leaving others with no or poor service.

involves only localized monopoly power in specific situations; instead, it involves a more generalized, market-wide market power. Such general market power may evolve because of economies-of-scale barriers to entry or, more frequently, entry controls. As will be discussed later, it is not clear that the minimum efficient scale of a taxi firm is very large, especially in a market highly dependent on cruising or street business. It is certainly larger in markets highly dependent on dispatch, contract, and concession business, and it would be even larger if fares had to be advertised other than on the sides of taxis. Under the latter conditions many smaller municipalities would find themselves with only one or two firms able to offer service profitably, and these municipalities may wish to regulate fares to control the concomitant market power.[10]

A more prevalent source of market power is the existence of entry controls. With a limited number of firms allowed to operate in a particular market, it is conceivable that in the absence of fare regulation they could collude (even tacitly) to raise fares and earn monopoly profits which would then be reflected in the values of their operating authorities (medallions or licences). Regulators could presumably regulate fares in this situation so that they just covered all economic costs, generated no monopoly profits, and conferred little or no value on the licences. The likelihood of such collusion diminishes as the number of firms in the industry increases,[11] however, and this rationale has little merit in and of itself in many of the larger metropolitan markets. Interestingly, this rationale, while it may appeal to some economists because of the existence of entry controls, appears to carry little weight with politicians and regulators since in nearly all markets with both entry and fare regulation, the licences carry with them a positive and sometimes high transfer price.

2 Analysis

The arguments in favour of fare regulation have considerable merit. The reduced information, transaction, and negotiation costs of regulated taxi fares, coupled with the increased consumer protection they offer, probably more than outweigh the social costs of having regulated fares. This argument is stronger if the regulated

---

10 This argument states, in essence, that in smaller municipalities there would be a natural monopoly in the taxi industry. I shall not enter the debate concerning the regulation of prices set by natural monopolies and merely note its existence. See H. Demsetz, 'Why regulate utilities?,' *Journal of Law and Economics*, 11, April 1968, and 'On the regulation of industry: a reply,' *Journal of Political Economy*, 79, March / April 1971; L.G. Telser, 'On the regulation of industry: a note,' Ibid., 77, November / December 1969, and rejoinder in Ibid., 79, March / April 1971; and O.E. Williamson, 'Franchise bidding for natural monopolies – in general and with respect to *CATV*,' *Bell Journal* 7:1, Spring 1976.

11 See G. Stigler, 'A theory of oligopoly,' *Journal of Political Economy* 72:1, February 1964.

fare structure can be automatically adjusted to encourage increased industry capacity during periods of normally peak or excess demand. It is further strengthened if there is relatively free entry so that variations in capacity can be readily provided. The argument must be qualified, however, with the condition that fares be regulated optimally or nearly so.

Identifying the socially desirable fare is a difficult task for most regulators. They have only imperfect information about the industry, and they are usually subjected to continual lobbying in one form or another by members of the industry; consequently there is a tendency for them to set fares too high. Among the cities studied below, Washington has been fortunate in having a weak industry lobby, stronger than usual regulators, and the countervailing power of business and government interests wishing to keep fares low. The success of their system in other cities would depend on the quality of the fare regulation that could be imposed in these cities. Of course the easiest solution to the problems set out above is to regulate only maximum fares. This type of regulation would have information and consumer protection benefits but would be less restrictive of market forces.

Entry regulation

1 Rationale
The case for entry regulation is usually based on four general considerations: (1) the reduction of negative externalities, such as congestion, pollution, noise, dangerous vehicles, and unsafe drivers; (2) consumer protection; (3) the generation of income for members of the industry; and (4) the stable provision of services. Those arguing that entry controls are necessary to reduce negative externalities have frequently stated that if there are fewer taxis in a market, there will be fewer of these problems as well. (They are implicitly assuming that there is a fixed-output-coefficients-joint-production function with the joint outputs of taxi services and the negative externalities.) In this view, the only way to reduce these externalities is to reduce the amount of taxi services provided. However, this argument is not sound. If noise is a problem, better mufflers and periodic vehicle inspection can be required. If pollution is a problem, better emission control devices, again coupled with periodic vehicle inspections, can be required.[12] If congestion is a problem, the specific causes of the congestion may provide a more efficient focal point for

12 It is even plausible that taxicabs generate considerably less pollution than many other forms of municipal passenger transportation: 'Many fallacies have developed concerning fuel-efficiency of taxicabs. When a trip involved five or less passengers, the taxicab is the most fuel-efficient method regardless of trip.' *Taxicab Management* 23:7, July 1975, 24. If there is a monotonic relationship between fuel consumption and pollution emission, the above quotation provides additional support against entry controls to reduce pollution.

regulation. For example, the number of taxis allowed at each particular taxi stand can be restricted or penalties against double parking and other parking violations can be enforced more strictly and severely. In addition, if there were free entry and a lower fare structure, congestion might even be reduced as the number of single-passenger private vehicles on the road declines. Finally, if driver and vehicle safety are of concern, minimum safety standards can be imposed.

The consumer protection arguments for entry control are similar in nature to the negative externality arguments. The important questions to answer are: what must consumers be protected from?, and what are the best ways to provide such protection? If consumers need to be protected from unconscionably high fares, fare regulation (not entry regulation) may help provide a solution. In fact, judging from the high licence values in some markets with restricted entry, entry control may have an adverse effect on consumer welfare. If consumers need to be protected from unsafe or criminal drivers, minimum driver standards can be imposed. Indeed such standards are imposed, even in cities with no entry controls. It may even be the case that entry controls inhibit the enforcement of restrictions designed to alleviate the problems of negative externalities or designed for consumer protection. If licences have high market values, regulators may frequently be more reluctant to punish offenders with licence revocation than they would be if licences have little or no market value. [13]

The third rationale for entry limitation arises, although not always very explicitly, from concern about the incomes of members of the industry (basically owners, owner-drivers, and non-owner drivers). Entry limitations are unlikely to increase the incomes of non-owner drivers except during adjustment periods; they make it possible for each taxi to earn more revenue, but this possibility increases the opportunity costs of the owners of the taxi licences. If the owners face a very elastic supply curve of drivers, drivers' net wages will not increase much, if at all, as a result of entry limitations, but the prices of licences will increase. [14] Drivers

13 In Toronto, this reluctance to punish by revocation often manifests itself in the requirement that an owner either sell his licence at the market price or have it revoked. In this manner serious or frequent violators of the law can be exorcised from the industry without imposing serious financial loss on them. Consequently, the appropriation of licences of high market value appears to be viewed as too harsh a punishment for nearly all crimes, and this possible enforcement tool has fallen into disuse in Toronto. Nevertheless, the requirement that such offenders leave the industry is still a viable enforcement tool, and allowing them to dispose of their assets at market prices may make Toronto regulators no more reluctant to use such a tool than they would be if licences had no market value.

14 An interesting example, which will be discussed in greater detail later, of the effects of entry limitations is provided by recent experience in London. Considerably stronger limitations were implemented concerning future entry without reducing the current number of licences, and licence values increased from about $1500 to about $2500 over a period of less than four months in anticipation of increased future revenues. In future, taxi and licence rental fees will probably increase more than drivers' wages.

might gain during a transition period as licence owners adjust rental fees or commissions more slowly than seems profitable. Rapidly changing fees and commissions may involve lost goodwill and lost driving time for owners, and so they may prefer to change these rates only for new drivers. Eventually, however, drivers' net wages should be competed back down at their original level. It is difficult, of course, to separate pleas for increased fares from pleas for additional entry limitations under this rationale, but the recent increase in entry controls in London, Ontario was justified primrily on the grounds of generating additional business for the owner-drivers, who constitute approximately 60 per cent of the London business. What most policy makers fail to recognize is that it is the owner who receives the benefits of such limitations.

A related argument often presented in favour of entry regulation is that without it the industry would devolve into cut-throat, chaotic competition. If there were no entry controls, it is said, taxi drivers would not be able to earn an honest living and would turn to dishonest activities in conjunction with their driving. There is no reason to believe that entry controls can help to solve this problem. With or without high licence values, taxi drivers will be in fairly competitive supply and will earn approximately the same net wages. If they are prone to engaging in illegal activities without entry limitations, they will be just as prone to do so with entry limitations.

The final argument favouring entry regulation is that if taxi owners did not have high licence values to 'protect,' they would not offer service during periods when they do not want to drive, such as during snow storms.[15] The implicit assumption that people will work harder if they have larger debts is like arguing that a person would work harder with a mortgaged house than with a rented home. It is not clear that such is the case; the pure wealth effect on the supply of labour is indeterminate. It is not clear, however, that even for licences worth $33,200, the interest costs at 11 per cent amount to less then $10 a day, and these daily costs are very small relative to the size of the debt.

A different variant of the above argument points out that the $10 / day interest costs on a licence exist primarily because with entry limitations a taxi can expect to gross $10 more a day than it could without entry limitations. Consequently, licence owners can expect to forgo $10 more every day their licences are not used. The

15 In Washington, where all drivers of taxis and private automobiles are required to have snow tires on their cars during snow alerts, many people, including taxi drivers, prefer not to drive rather than to invest in snow tires for the few times a year they are required. Consequently, at the regulated fares the demand for taxi services increases while the supply decreases during snow alerts, creating periods of considerable excess quantity demanded. Of course, this excess quantity demanded could be eliminated if taxis were allowed to charge a premium during snow alerts. Currently the only way they are able to charge such a premium is by charging each passenger in a group the full fare as opposed to the usual 50 cents charged for additional passengers in a group.

opportunity costs of their leisure time or of avoiding unpleasant driving conditions are greater than would be the case if there were no entry limitations. As we shall see, if taxi licence owners are receiving only a normal rate of return on their licences, their decision whether to drive during a particular brief period of adverse conditions will be affected only by substitution effects, not income effects. The substitution effects, if they exist, will encourage owners to make greater use of their licences under adverse conditions than would otherwise be made, so that entry controls will encourage the provision of more service than would otherwise be provided.

This variant of the argument has three major flaws. The first, and most obvious, is that while entry controls may encourage a larger proportion of licence owners to provide service, this will be a larger proportion of a smaller number of taxis; there could be a larger actual number, despite the smaller proportion of taxis providing service under adverse conditions with free entry as opposed to limited entry. As an example, suppose that with free entry a given city could have 3000 taxis, but with limited entry it has only 2500. If 60 per cent of the limited-entry taxis were to provide service under adverse conditions but only 50 per cent of the free-entry taxis did so, there would be no difference in the amount of taxi service offered.

The second flaw in the argument is that it assumes that under adverse conditions limited-entry taxis could still earn a premium relative to free-entry taxis. Such may well not be the case. It is quite conceivable (perhaps plausible is a better word) that under such conditions all taxis on the road will be able to operate at full capacity and generate exactly the same receipts during the period. Such conditions may do more than generate an additional excess quantity demanded for the limited-entry taxis, but they cannot capitalize on this additional excess quantity demanded so long as fares are regulated. With the controlled-entry premium considerably reduced or eradicated, the substitution effect is also substantially reduced or eliminated, and limited entry may guarantee no better service than would be provided by taxis with free entry.

Even if a small premium did exist, and even if it did provide sufficient incentives for licence owners under limited entry to provide more taxi service than would be provided with free entry, it may not be socially desirable to have such a result. Certainly the consumers of taxi services would benefit, but the remainder of the community may be harmed if having too many vehicles on the streets generates negative externalities, such as congestion during a snowstorm.

2 Analysis

The theoretical arguments for entry regulation are thus unconvincing. Among the cities studied, Washington shows that free entry can work well. Certainly if the quality of fare regulation in some cities is low, there is no reason to expect entry regulation to rectify the situation. Low-quality fare regulation will generally go hand in hand with low-quality entry regulation from society's point of view, and the situation could quite conceivably be made even worse.

In London in November 1977, the implicit rental price of a licence was approximately \$280 / year, and each taxi made approximately 7000 trips / year, so that entry regulation generated somewhat less than 4 cents per trip of average length. Because open market licence prices were so low, it is unfortunate that the city moved towards tighter entry regulation rather than looser entry regulation. Those holding licences at that time would have suffered little capital loss from a gradual move to free entry, and the city would have laid the basis for a more flexible taxicab industry. At the regulated fares, it is unlikely that more than four or five additional full-time equivalent taxis would have entered the industry, but a greater use of part-time and seasonal taxis could well have ensued, providing London with increased taxi service during periods of peak demand and causing less concern during the slack period. If, at the same time, the city had reduced fares by 4 cents on the average, licence values would have been completely eroded, but no permanent exit would have taken place.

Though there will not likely be fewer taxis per resident in London in future, as costs increase fares could be held constant and implicit licence rental values could be eroded. Such a policy would be at best a poor approximation to the competitive norm. Although it would reduce or eliminate the monopoly rents conferred by the city, it will not necessarily yield the price-output configuration that is socially desirable. Certainly reduced fares with free entry as a policy has as much to recommend it and probably more, since it would encourage more flexible capacity in the industy over time.[16]

The relatively low prices of taxicab owners' licences in London indicates that there is (and has been) considerable capacity flexibility or at least capacity utilization flexibility, even with restricted entry. This flexibility comes from double shifting and from the section of the bylaw which permits owners to leave their licences dormant for up to 120 days without revocation. The licence value in London has been determined exclusively by the effect entry restriction had on single shifting; free entry by licence owners into double shifting competed the return to double shifting down to zero.

As time passes in London, not only will each single-shifted cab have more trips a year, but the returns to double shifting will also increase. And to the extent that double shifting involves some managerial economies of scale, fleet owners and

16 The basic problem with such policy changes, of course, is that they impose a capital loss on current members of the industry who may well have paid high prices for licences and be earning little more than a normal return on their investments. This problem will be discussed later in greater detail.

brokers will gain control of, if not ownership of, an increasing number of licences. This will reduce flexibility in the London industry and increase the concentration of control within the industry.

A pattern emerges: in Washington there is free entry, little double shifting, considerable capacity flexibility, and very low licence values; in London there are some entry restrictions set in such a manner that there has been some double shifting, some capacity flexibility, and moderately low licence values; and in Toronto there are strict entry controls, almost complete double shifting, and high licence values, and the only capacity flexibility is provided by bandit cabs.

To the extent that entry regulation reduces apparent excess capacity in the taxicab industry, it might be deemed desirable by even some disinterested observers. It must be recognized, however, that having cabs off the streets much of the time does not necessarily represent excess capacity in the sense of wasted resources. Less intensive cab utilization extends their expected lifetimes so that the capacity is usable for a longer period of time. Furthermore, to the extent that off-duty taxis are used as personal vehicles, as is prevalent in Washington, this apparent excess capacity is no greater (and probably less) than might be observed among strictly family cars. The advantage of free entry and widespread part-time participation in the industry is that, as demand conditions change either predictably or unpredictably, the supply of taxi services can change relatively quickly in response to those changes in market conditions.

The transitional gains trap[17]

The net social benefits of having free entry into taxicab industries should be clear by now. Customers would receive more frequent service, perhaps at lower prices; capacity would be more flexible and would respond more quickly to market conditions; members of the industry would face lower barriers to exit, generating greater overall resource mobility; and there would be reduced social costs of administering the remaining regulations. Nevertheless, deregulating industries which currently have entry controls would impose in some cases enormous capital losses on some members of the industry As Tullock points out:

> By now, the capital value of the monopoly profit has been fully taken into account in the industry. New entrants enter only by purchasing the medallion, with the result that they get only normal profits. Further, the surviving original owners have opportunity costs equivalent to the value of the medallions upon which they receive normal returns. The customers, of course, are worse off.
>
> Can we suggest a compensation scheme which would get us out of the mess? Normally, the answer to this question is no, because the implied transaction costs are excessive. If we

17 This term is taken from an article with the same title by G. Tullock, *Bell Journal of Economics*, 6:2, Autumn 1975.

could somehow identify those people who are now not using a cab but would at a slightly lower price and tax them it would be possible to gradually buy back the monopoly from its current owners, and hence benefit everyone. Unfortunately, we have no way of doing it, and hence my reference to the situation as being an 'inefficient point on the Paretian frontier.'[18]

Furthermore, any scheme, to be totally compensatory, must also compensate those on the new issue waiting list for perhaps working in the industry at less than their opportunity-cost wages in anticipation of receiving large future capital gains.

One possible method for freeing ourselves from the taxicab transitional gains trap would be for the licensing commission to rent licences annually for some value approximating their current market rental value with due allowance for the increased liquidity and resource flexibility provided by such a scheme. Under this scheme, licences in Toronto might rent for $4000 and in London for $300. There would be essentially no limit on the number of licences rented, and those currently owning licences would be required to pay only the current renewal fees. To compensate those on waiting lists, the scheme should perhaps not be implemented until all those currently on such lists have received their licences.

While the scheme would not necessarily make current consumers better off, it would also make current owners no worse off. Furthermore, the collection of the annual licence rentals over time (perhaps a very long time for Toronto) would enable the licensing commissions eventually to compensate fully all persons who might suffer a capital loss from entry deregulation. When sufficient revenues have been collected, the compensation can be paid, entry can be deregulated to the benefit of future consumers and members of society, and none of the immediately apparent capital losses would occur. Such a scheme might, however, impose some unmeasured losses: some current brokers and fleet managers might have to find alternative employment because free entry would likely encourage more part-time involvement in the industry and reduce the demand for their services.

Case studies

At first glance it appears that an unregulated taxicab industry in a reasonably sized municipality would be monopolistically competitive. If the municipality is large enough, there would be many taxicabs in it relative to the demand, and one might assume that there would be very little interdependence of economic decision-making. Furthermore, because the start-up costs of operating a taxicab are relatively low, one might also be led to believe there would be fairly free entry into the industry. To some extent these conclusions are correct.

As one studies the industry more closely, however, one becomes impressed with the significance of scheduling and dispatching. These activities have rather substantial economies of scale in lower output ranges and tend to create more

18 Ibid., 672.

concentrated, oligopolistic industries, especially in smaller municipalities. Consequently some local taxicab industries, in the absence of regulations, have evolved into oligopolistic industries, sometimes with a competitive fringe of independent, unaffiliated taxis. These industries may still have unconcentrated licence ownership patterns, but the brokerage and dispatching operations have become concentrated in only a few firms.

1 London, Ontario

The City of London regulates the fare structure of, and entry into, its taxicab industry. In June 1977, fares were raised over the objections of some members of the industry. Those objecting did so for two reasons. First, those firms concentrating on house phone-in business rather than contract business feared a substantial reduction in business resulting from the fare increase as their clients increasingly turned to the use of the public transportation system. Second, some objectors to the fare increase appear to have done so more in public than in private in an attempt to use their objection as advertising. City council was persuaded to increase fares partially by the observation that a taxi fare increase would generate additional bus ridership, reducing the necessary subsidy to the bus system.

Until early 1978, taxis could also be hired per hour rather than per mile. This hourly rate was used by some firms to calculate their bids for contracts, enabling them to submit bids below those submitted by firms basing their bids on meter readings. This strategy was particularly important to those firms foreseeing a weak future in the cruising business and the house-and-bar business. The hourly rate was removed from the fare structure in early 1978 at the urging of a majority of the firms in the industry. Clearly, for the industry as a whole, it has been perceived that contract business has a fairly inelastic demand, so that raising the fares on this business will not reduce its volume very much. Eliminating the hourly rate thus serves two purposes: it cuts off one avenue for price cutting, and it enables the other taxi firms to gain a better idea of appropriate bids to be tendered. In other words, it reduces the dimensions of competition by nearly eliminating price competition, and it forces contractors (e.g. the post office and school systems) to decide between competing bids on other grounds, such as the provision of an acceptable level of service.

The City of London attempts to licence taxicabs so that there will be one taxi for approximately every 1350 residents. This ratio was changed in early 1978 from one taxi per 970 residents, and the industry sources predict that new licences will not be issued again until 1984 or 1985. No licences were withdrawn by the city at the time of the ratio change, so that it had no immediate impact on revenues earned per taxicab. In the past, new licences were issued only once each year and then only if the population had increased sufficiently to allow the issuance of four new licences. In the seven years from 1972 to 1978 only sixteen new licences were issued. They were issued in groups of four in the order in which names appeared on a waiting list; two to non-owner drivers, one to an owner, and one to a broker. The recent ratio change has significantly reduced the implicit value of having one's name high on the current waiting list.

The issue price of a licence was $200 with a renewal fee of $20 / year. Licences can be transferred in the open market suject to a number of conditions, the more significant of which include: (1) a $200 transfer fee must be paid to the city; (2) the purchaser must have been a licensed taxi driver on a full-time basis for at least one year; (3) the vendor must have operated the licence for at least one year; and (4) no purchaser may acquire more than two licences during any calendar year. In November 1977 the transfer price of a licence was approximately $1500. As of June 1978 with the expected future change in the ratio of taxis to residents, licences sold for approximately $2500. By 1984 the price was over $4000.

London requires for consumer protection that taxis be mechanically fit, that drivers know the city and its bylaws, that taximeters be regularly inspected, and that each taxi have at least $300,000 liability insurance. All the bylaws are made and subject to change by City Council, generally at the instigation of a taxi liaison committee via a committee of City Council. The liaison committee consists of a broker, an owner, and a driver from each of the major firms in the city. Its meetings are held at most once a month and are chaired by the chief taxicab inspector for the city police.

In 1980 there were 252 taxi licences issued by the city. The bylaws provide that a licence may be kept dormant at City Hall for up to 120 days, a possibility sometimes used by owners to avoid paying insurance during the slower summer months. In November 1977 six licences were dormant at City Hall; in January 1978 all licences were in service because winter generates good business for taxis in London. In June 1978 252 licences were owned by about 125 different firms or individuals. The owner of the largest number of licences owned no more than about 35 of them, but some firms controlled more licences through family licence ownership and other formal or informal arrangements.

This relatively high concentration of licence control and affiliation evolved for two reasons. The first is that there are economies of scale in fleet management. Maintaining a list of drivers and maintaining a fleet of vehicles involves numerous costs, many of which can be reduced (per taxi) by consolidating them. The second reason is that most of the taxi business in London is phone-in and dispatch business or contract business; no more than 20 per cent of the business is street or cruising business. To the extent that there are economies of scale in dispatching and contract negotiating relative to the size of the market, there will be a concentration of taxicab affiliations with brokers.

Because of the uncertainty about the future of the London taxi business, because of the recent ratio change, and because of the lags in adjustment to new market conditions imposed by regulations, current licence values do not provide a very good estimate of current economic rents accruing to licence owners. For this estimate, November 1977 data were used. This was a period during which one major operator appeared to be in financial trouble and in which there was no indication that the city would be willing to change the ratio of licences to residents. At that time, the consensus in the industry was that licences were being bought and sold for around $1500.[19]

On average, a taxi could gross $60 / shift in London in 1978. This figure is an annual average, and accounts for dull summer afternoons as well as busy winter weekend evenings. An owner driving his own car generally works slightly more than five shifts a week on average, or 280 shifts per year. Consequently, his reported receipts for the year will be $16,800. Such an owner / driver had on average total direct expenses of $9820 per year, leaving a net revenue of $6980 plus tips per year as a return to labour, entrepreneurship, and ownership of his licence. Since he could receive tips plus 40 per cent of $16,800 (or $6720) by driving on commission, the net return to his entrepreneurship and licence ownership was about $260 per year. Given that licences cost $1500 plus a $200 transfer fee in November 1977, the owners were receiving about 16 per cent on their investment in licences then.

Discussions with members of the industry about double shifting yielded a variety of information. Some said that they could keep their cars on the road around the clock, while others said that finding a reliable second driver was not worth the trouble. One fairly reliable source said that double-shifted cars averaged about $21,000 a year in gross reported receipts, implying an average additional 70 shifts a year that a taxi could be rented. In view of the transient nature of second drivers and the seasonality of the business, this figure does not seem unreasonable.

Because brokers own so many of the licences in London, they form an important part of the market for licences. Assuming they got 60 per cent of the gross receipts and were able to rent their cars for an average of 350 shifts a year at $60 a shift, their average revenue was $12,600 a year per taxicab. There is some question whether concession fees are an expense for brokers with integrated

---

19 There is some seasonal fluctuation in licence prices, with lower prices in the summer than in the winter. This fluctuation occurs for at least two reasons: (1) business is considerably better in the winter, creating fewer cash flow problems than for potential purchasers (this is particularly important for potential purchasers with low net worth and who might be subject to credit rationing in imperfect capital markets); (2) insurance premium increases are generally announced near the end of the summer, and uncertainty about the new rates puts downward pressure on transfer prices.

operations, but the answer seems to be that rates of return are similar for brokers and owner-drivers; if they were not, market transactions would take place until they were.

While the returns to London taxicab licences are perhaps greater than what many economists would consider to be 'normal' returns, they are perhaps understandable in view of the nature of the London business. First, there is a fairly thin market for licences, with few transactions taking place in any given period; if someone faced a personal liquidity crisis, selling the licence on short notice could prove very difficult. Second, there is a risk of uninsured collision damages to one's car. Third, there is a risk that London might not have bad weather in any given year. Fourth, there is a risk of future insurance premium changes. And fifth, there is a risk (albeit small) that city regulations might change adversely for the industry. These risks seem high enough to suggest that, if anything, the returns to licence ownership have been underestimated. Perhaps this underestimation arises because the calcualtions are based on reported revenues instead of actual revenues and expected future revenues.

Why don't Londoners with a preference for risks buy licences, if they can return more than 16 per cent a year? The answer, basically, is that there are some substantial barriers to entry. To become a licence owner one must have been licensed as a driver for at least two years and have driven on a permanent basis for at least one year; furthermore, in order to use the licence one must be a driver or a broker, since the rental market for licences is virtually non-existent. Becoming a broker is next to impossible in London, with the broker's market probably already overcrowded. Becoming a driver may be unattractive to many people who might have to forgo a higher salary in a different occupation. These barriers, while by no means insurmountable, are substantial enough to limit the downward competitive pressure on licence rates of return.

2 Toronto

Toronto, like London, regulates both fares and entry into its taxicab industry. Fares per mile are set; hourly rates can be negotiated. Entry is limited so there will be approximately one taxi for every 875 residents. New licences are issued once a year: 70 per cent to non-owning drivers, 10 per cent to owners of one licence, 10 per cent to owners of two to nine licences, and 10 per cent to owners of ten or more licences. The new issue price of a licence is $1000 to a non-owning driver and $5000 to current owners; the renewal fee is $220 annually.

Bylaw changes in Toronto are usually initiated by members of the industry, who present briefs to the Metropolitan Licensing Commission, which in turn makes recommendations to the Council of the Municipality of Metropolitan Toronto.

Generally, the Toronto bylaw seems to be designed to erect high barriers to both entry and exit. For example, a non-owner of any licence must be a full-time driver, dispatcher, or fleet manager for at least three consecutive years before he can even have his name placed on the waiting list to receive a licence, and each year that his name is on the waiting list he must file a number of income and employment documents with the commission verifying his full-time employment. With the current waiting period of at least four years, someone must work in the industry for at least seven years before receiving a licence. A current owner of one or more licences may remain on one of the owner's waiting lists only if he has not sold any licences during the preceding five years; and if the purchase of any additional licence(s) disqualifies a person from being on one waiting list, he moves to or near the bottom of the appropriate waiting list. Finally, once a licence is issued, it may not be sold and the taxicab and licence may not be leased to someone else for at least five years except for such compassionate grounds as disability or death.

These barriers leave potential entrants with a long expected waiting period or the option of purchasing licences in the open market. And once a new licence has been issued to someone, that person is very reluctant to leave the industry for at least five years for fear of having a valuable licence revoked. Consequently, although there are large potential capital gains to be earned on Toronto taxicab licences, people must generally be in the industry for at least twelve years before these gains can be realized. And once the gains are realized, anyone selling a licence may not purchase a different one even on the open market for at least five years. A further impediment is that after a person is issued his first new licence, not only is he prohibited from selling or leasing it, but also he must be either a regular driver of that taxicab or a regular dispatcher to keep the licence.

It seems that part of the strategy of these impediments is to keep licences (and the attendant capital gains) largely in the hands of drivers or owners of one licence. Another part of the strategy seems to be a desire to restrict speculation in taxicab licences. This strategy is apparently working. The January 1975 data show that of 1372 licence owners, 1123 were single-licence owners; of all licences outstanding, single-licence owners held about 50 per cent. The data for 1978 indicate that the major growth in licence ownership has been among single-licence owners.

Despite these barriers to entry and exit, because Toronto is a large city and because the Toronto taxi industry is a large industry, there is still a brisk trade in taxi licences. Formally, the commission terminates the seller's licence and issues a new one to the purchaser, but this formality means no more than that all sales are made subject to the approval of the commission. Consequently, the commission has detailed records of each transaction. Licence prices have been steadily increasing; from January 1973 to Spring 1978 the average price of a licence increased from $18–20,000 to $26,500. Strictly speaking, a licence cannot be traded by itself: the transaction must include a fully equipped vehicle. However, the vehicles included in the transactions frequently are near the end of their expected lifetime, so the data reflect fairly accurately the value of a licence. These numbers do not, however, include several transaction prices such as 'one dollar plus love and affection' which accompanied sales within a family.

The taxicab business in Toronto is spread more evenly over a 24-hour period than it is in London. Day shifts can involve a high percentage of message and small parcel delivery for downtown business.[20] And the night life in Toronto is active enough to provide considerable business for night shift drivers. Dispatching is less important in Toronto than in London, with no more than 50 to 55 per cent of the business being phone-in. In fact, the independent taxi owners generally operate without radios. Dispatching in most firms is done on what is known as a bid system. When a call is received by a dispatching office, the dispatcher radios for available cars in a particular region to tell him their locations, and then he gives the call to the cab closest to it. Because the dispatchers do not have to keep priority lists of cabs in each region, each dispatcher can handle more calls and more taxicabs, and the dispatching costs are slightly lower per call. Therefore the minimum efficient scale is slightly higher than it would be if the priority dispatch system were used. Typically the major dispatching firms in Toronto have about one dispatcher for 90 cabs during peak periods, while in London they have one dispatcher for 60 cabs during peaks. But it must also be remembered that Toronto dispatchers, even in peak periods, are handling fewer calls per cab. Because of these dispatching economies of scale, there is some concentration in the brokerage aspect of the industry, but due to the size of the market, the concentration is less than it is in London.

Concession fees are generally lower in Toronto than in London for several reasons. First, there is less phone-in business per cab in Toronto and more cruising business, making the dispatching costs per cab lower. Second, there is more competition for owners among the brokers, keeping the concession fees down. And third, there are no broker-specific exclusive concessions and a smaller proportion of contract business in Toronto than in London. This last reason, through, is offset somewhat by greater use of direct phone lines to various apartments, hotels, and other buildings in Toronto.

The federal government has recently implemented a new system governing taxicab service to Toronto International Airport. In 1980 there was a limit of 300 licences for taxis to operate at the airport, 68 of which were obtained by taxis from Metro Toronto. The licences cost $875 in 1979 and were allocated randomly, but

20 For drivers choosing to concentrate on the downtown area during the day, message and small parcel delivery can account for as much as 60 to 70 per cent of their trips and 80 to 85 per cent of their receipts.

the cost of airport licences was expected to rise as the extent of the excess demand for them became apparent. Prior to the implementation of the current scheme, taxis were charged 25 cents per pickup to cover traffic management costs at the airport. The new scheme serves to reduce taxicab congestion at the airport and extracts a large monopoly rent from the taxis serving the airport. It is also believed by some that the new scheme will reduce the incidence of 'fare selection' whereby a driver, having waited for an hour or so, refuses to take someone on a short trip.

A major problem in Toronto is the large number of unlicensed bandit cabs operating there. The bandits form three distinct groups. The first consists of taxicabs from the suburbs that drive a passenger to Toronto and stay there picking up street business for awhile before returning to the suburbs. The second is limousines that pick up and discharge passengers within the Metro city limits. The third group of bandit cabs is made up of current Toronto licence owners who operate more than one taxi on one licence. The taxi plate numbers must match the vehicle numbers, but frequently plates are 'lost' or damaged in accidents, or else spare plates are issued for a different vehicle while the originally licensed one is being repaired. In all of these cases, the owners can then illegally operate more than one vehicle with the same number, using one licence for all of them. Some sources estimate that there are as many as 500 to 600 bandits operating in Toronto.

The operation of bandits in Toronto, but not in London, is by no means surprising. Judging from the differences in licence prices, there is much more business available per taxi in Toronto than in London. Also, the barriers to legitimate entry are considerably higher in Toronto. It is to be expected that as the costs of legitimate entry increase and the benefits from illegitimate entry also increase, there will be more bandit cab activity.

It is illegal to lease only the taxi licence in Toronto; an owner must lease an equipped and insured car along with the licence. This prohibition on leasing is circumvented, however, by numerous people. Apparently a lessee purchases and insures a car in the lessor's name, or else the lessee leases the car to the licence owner and leases it back again with the plate attached. Estimates suggest licence owners can lease their licences for approximately 13 per cent a year. Although no single economic agent owns more than thirty-two licences in Toronto, press reports and interviews have indicated that some people control many more licences than they own, perhaps as many as 200 licences. It is most likely to be the managers who control a large number of licences who lease some of them, presumably to drivers waiting to purchase their own licences or waiting for their names to come up to the top of the new-issue list. Sources estimate that hundreds of Toronto licences are leased.

The return to a licence can also be calculated on the basis that the owner drives his car during one shift and rents it during another. Assume that each taxi is in operation, on the average, for 560 shifts a year or 280 days with two shifts a day. If so, the total revenue is $15,120 and the total costs (excluding the opportunity costs of the licence and the management of it) are $10,190. The return to a licence is $4210 per year, or slightly over 15 per cent a year for an owner-driver renting his taxi out for a second shift or for an owner renting his car for two shifts per day.

In Toronto, unlike in London, owners can readily double shift their cabs on a regular basis, in part because there are smaller daily, weekly, fortnightly, month-ly, and seasonal cycles in the demand for taxi services in Toronto, but apparently also because of differences in licensing policies between the two municipalities. London seems to have licensed enough taxis to provide full-time business for the licence owners during peak periods and to allow licences to remain dormant during off-peak periods. These off-peak periods are substantial enough that taxis gener-ally cannot be double shifted on a full-time basis. In Toronto, however, there appears to be a policy of licencing only enough taxis to provide sufficient business for licencees double shifting their cabs even during off-peak periods. Then during the peak periods bandits are more likely to come on the scene, to the relief of the waiting customers.

3 Washington, DC

Washington regulates taxicab fares, but not entry in any broad sense, making it unique among other major cities in North America.[21] Fares are based on the number of zones crossed while the cab is under hire, so that the cabs do not have taximeters. While zone pricing eliminates the meter costs for taxi owners, it also leads to the interesting phenomena of some fairly expensive short trips and some fairly inexpensive long trips. It also means that residents of the District, who generally know the zones quite well, frequently walk a block or two to save by not crossing into an additional zone while in the cab. Because visitors don't know the zones, there is a strong possibility that they frequently pay higher fares than they should.

Trips originating or ending outside the District, such as trips to Dulles or the National Airport, were charged at 65¢ a mile in 1978. Drivers generally seem to prefer these trips, as evidenced by their willingness to join lengthy queues at the airports. Generally the District attempts to impose cost-of-service pricing, allow-ing surcharges for telephone-radio business, for increased driving times during the evening rush hour, and for various forms of personal service.[22] There are two notable and related exceptions to this general policy. First, all taxis are permitted to

21 Some people in London and Toronto have referred to Washington as the 'bastard of the industry.'
22 Usually additional passengers with the same origin and destination are charged 50 cents apiece. During snow emergencies, however, all passengers in a group are charged the single-passenger fare.

provide a jitney service, picking up and discharging passengers along or near a route and charging each of them the full fare. Each passenger is charged the full fare presumably because of the problems of allocating a total fare to different passengers with different origins and destinations. The result is that even with a passenger drivers carefully scan the streets because the marginal revenue of picking up additional passengers is positive and the marginal cost is near zero. The second exception is that taxis delivering messages or small parcels must do so within three hours from when they are picked up (unless some urgency is declared) but also must pick up passengers if flagged down while the item to be delivered is in the vehicle. This requirement is in direct opposition to that in Toronto which provides that taxis engaged for delivery may not pick up passengers until the delivery has been made.

Fare regulation with free entry is no easier than fare regulation with restricted entry. If fares are set too high, there will be too many cabs in the industry and excess capacity. If fares are set too low there will be exit from the industry by all but those with the lowest opportunity costs. The Public Service Commission has set zone boundaries and charges in an attempt to provide drivers with a net return of about $3.50 per hour. Doing so has been difficult for them since they do not have accurate cost and revenue data. While the data provided to the regulatory agency might usually be shaded to the benefit of industry members, leading to regulated fares above the competition level, Washington has considerable pressure on it by the government and its lobbyists to maintain low fares. These countervailing influences seem to have provided fares near the competitive level, although considerable exits from the industry in 1978–9 indicate that fares may be lagging behind cost increases.

Although there is free entry into the Washington taxi industry, there are numerous minor entry controls designed primarily for consumer protection. In addition to driver and vehicle safety standards, each taxi must be insured. The required insurance, however, is considerably less than is required in either London or Toronto. Consequently, the perceived insurance costs in Washington are also considerably lower, amounting to $11-13 per week or about $600 a year per taxicab in 1978. Taxi owners are liable for all uninsured damages, but a standard assumption in the industry is that if such damages were ever required to be paid, the liable person would most likely leave town or declare personal bankruptcy.

With free entry and relatively low overhead expenses, a large number (65 – 70 per cent) of taxi owners drive only part time. For such owners the taxicab is also a personal car, painted and with a roof light. Fares are accepted on the way to work in the morning and for several hours after a regular job in the afternoon; the car is insured the entire time under the taxi insurance; and most, if not all, of its operating costs can be considered as business expenses for tax purposes. Furthermore, because there are no taximeters and nearly all transactions are on a cash basis, substantial portions of the incomes can be hidden, again for tax purposes.[23] Hence, part-time driving is fairly lucrative for many owners there.[24]

Dispatching in Washington accounts for a very small portion of the business; less than 25 per cent of the taxis have radios, and even for those that do, a sizeable majority of the business is still non-radio business.

As a result of the free entry, the predominantly part-time nature of the industry, and the nature of the demand for taxi services in Washington, there are many more taxis licenced per resident there than either Toronto or London. There were approximately 7500 cars licenced as of December 1977. There is some feeling among many in the industry that the opening of the subway and its extension, particularly to National Airport, has cut into the taxi business somewhat, and this could account for some of the reduction in the number of cabs licensed in recent years.

Although the street business is good in Washington, most of the taxi owners are affiliated with a fleet or an association. Associations can offer, in varying degrees, discount or free towing, discount and / or no-interest repairs, exclusive concession rights, direct phone lines and dispatching service, general management services to reduce red tape for the owners, and / or free or discount legal advice. The association fees vary with the amount of service offered by the association.

There are two basic types of cab owners in Washington, and perhaps elsewhere too. Some prefer to hustle the street business and cruise a lot; others prefer to wait longer between trips at the airports or at exclusive concessions for longer trips. These preferences to some extent determine the association an owner will join and also help to determine how much an association is willing to pay for an exclusive concession. There is some industry opposition to exclusive concessions. The existence of exclusive concessions can have a tendency to increase concentration in an industry, because large associations can (at least in the short run) afford to bid high prices and spread the costs over many owners in the association. Since there are relatively few valuable exclusive concessions in Washington, this tendency

23 Several owners responded to our questions by asking, 'Are you sure you're from Canada and not from the I.R.S.?' When some were asked point blank about the amount of tax cheating in the industry they responded, 'No comment.' One manager did point out, though, that tax investigators can check on people's personal expenses (e.g., apartment, food), and so tax cheating was limited by the fear of this investigation and possible subsequent prosecution.
24 The prevalence of the part-time owner-driver in Washington is reminiscent of the prairie farmers who continued to use horses long after tractors became more cost-efficient for farm work. A major reason they kept their horses was that the animals could be used to provide family transportation in addition to field work. In both cases, overlooking the joint use to be made of a means of transportation leads people to conclude incorrectly that such decision are economically irrational or involve inordinately high subjective personal benefits.

toward concentration has had little impact on the industry. As long as concentration is kept in check by other competitive forces, the major benefactors of the exclusive concession agreements are the hotel owners and managers. Their room rates would probably not be much different in the absence of exclusive concessions since cabs would still sit on the most desirable taxi stands, and so their customers would probably derive little benefit from the abolition of exclusive concessions. Some drivers may benefit from the concessions and be willing to pay to have the competition for this type of business limited. Other drivers who prefer taxi stands, however, must utilize the airports and the less busy hotels. Prohibiting exclusive concessions in Washington as has been done in Toronto might hurt some taxi owners and some hotel owners, but it might benefit some of the other owners in the industry by allowing them more freedom to provide taxi service in accordance with their personal preferences.

The radio business in Washington, as mentioned, is not a major portion of the total business. The primary reason for this situation is that with free entry cabs are generally plentiful, and most potential customers on or near moderately busy streets need wait only a few minutes at the most to hail a cruising cab. The simultaneity problem here has not received complete recognition in the theoretical literature: with limited entry, taxis might be able to do more street business than with free entry, but then customers would have longer waiting periods before being able to employ one. Rather than wait, some customers would prefer to telephone for a radio-dispatched taxi, thereby reducing the volume of street business, reducing the incentive of drivers to ply the streets as opposed to having radios, further increasing the expected waiting time for potential street customers, and so on. Consequently, entry limitations in Washington could have little effect on increasing radio business there; instead, they would probably mean higher costs to the passengers, longer average waiting times, and increased concentration of the industry to handle the increased radio business. Alternatively, if entry were *not* limited in Toronto, the industry would quite likely be very similar to the one in Washington with more street business, shorter waiting periods, perhaps less concentration, and possibly lower fares.

The above analysis overlooks one problem sometimes experienced in Washington. If a radio driver agrees to accept a call but then is flagged down on the street, he may continue to ply the streets and forget about the call, which significantly increases the expected waiting period for radio customers. Although some dispatching services have internal policing and punishment systems in order to discourage this practice in order to maintain good reputations, the problem persists. The solution, of course, is not to restrict entry to protect the radio customers but rather to implement and enforce stiffer penalties against such practices.

Washington taxi owners with radios generally do not have them for the purpose of revenue generation; they estimate that the revenues earned from radio calls just about offset the costs of having a radio. They perceive additional benefits from having a radio. First, the radio is viewed, especially by night drivers, as a lifeline, a safety or insurance measure, offering some protection against crime. Second, radios help them avoid speeding tickets because the dispatcher informs them of the location of radar.

With the apparent decline in business in Washington and the decline in the number of licensed taxis, the associations are scrambling for members. It is likely that some of the associations will not be able to survive. While the dying associations may primarily be small ones, the demise of some larger associations is not at all unlikely.

The Washington taxi industry is able to provide such generally good service on the whole, in part because of free entry and zone pricing. In part, however, the high quality of service is also the result of two important but indirect subsidies. One of the subsidies is from all American taxpayers to the Washington taxi consumers. If free entry and zone pricing facilitate widespread tax cheating in Washington, the consumers there have more frequent taxi service, shorter waiting periods, and higher quality drivers and vehicles than they would if there were less tax cheating.

The second subsidy is from those injured by liable taxi owners to taxi service customers. One reason that fares and waiting periods are low in Washinton is that explicit insurance costs are low. However, people who claim damages in excess of $10,000 due to a taxi owner's liability are often out of luck in Washington. Although the residents of Washington may wish to bear these uninsured risks in order to keep fares and waiting times low, it must be recognized that their agreeing to do so also involves an indirect subsidy to those who never suffer damages greater than $10,000.

4 Sarnia

Like Washington, Sarnia regulates fares but not entry into its taxicab industry. Mileage fares are set; hourly fares are available for group passengers. These fares are maximum fares, but none of the firms charges less.

Until 1977 there was an unofficial quota in Sarnia, limiting the number of taxicab licences to forty-eight (approximately one per 1000 residents in the mid-1970s). Even by the end of 1977 this quota had not been reached, but as it was approached cab licences took on a small positive value. It was discovered that the Police Commission (the appropriate regulatory body) had no legal authority to establish a quota, and the commission itself appeared to be uneasy about having one as the demand for new licences grew, and so in early 1978 the quota was raised to sixty-five (i.e. made ineffective again).

Despite the similarities in regulations between Sarnia and Washington – fare regulation with free entry – the industries are organized quite differently. Sarnia has fewer taxis per resident and has only three firms. Population size and density clearly affect the industry structures by reducing the expected profitability of cruising in Sarnia. Roughly speaking, cruising accounts for no more than 5 per cent of the Sarnia taxi business, contract business for about 15 per cent, telephone-dispatch for the remainder. What this comparison emphasizes is that free entry, in and of itself, will not necessarily lead to a deconcentrated low-fare industry. There are some 'multiplant' economies associated with dispatching and contract negotiation which lead to concentrated industries in low population density municipalities such as Sarnia.

Dispatching in Sarnia is very labour-intensive. The dispatchers not only receive calls and dispatch taxis, they also keep detailed records of pick-up points, destinations, times and fares for each dispatched trip. Clearly, the dispatchers are a fixed factor of production at such small scales of operation, and by keeping detailed records they are able to reduce the amount of cheating on fares which might be done by drivers who are paid on a commission basis. In other words, the marginal costs of keeping such records are near zero and doing so does have some benefits for the firm.

5   Windsor

As in Sarnia, there is relatively free entry into Windsor's taxicab industry, and, as in most medium-sized municipalities, the industry is highly concentrated, being dominated in Windsor by two large firms. Entry restrictions that do apply in Windsor address only vehicle and driver standards. Mileage fares are set, as is a per-hour group fare.

In Windsor, as in most other municipalities, the members of the industry are dependent on the telephone-dispatch business, with no more than 10 per cent of their gross revenues derived from cruising. This condition, coupled with the economies of scale in dispatching and negotiations, undoubtedly is the driving force which gives rise to the concentration of the firms in Windsor. In the fall of 1978, there were four companies operating 202 taxicabs and six independents.

All the Windsor firms sell insurance to their owner-drivers, a type of vertical integration uncommon in Ontario. Apparently most owner-drivers in Windsor prefer having the firms insure them on a group basis. Another interesting feature of the Windsor industry is the survival of the six independents. Most of these men are older and have built up a consistent clientele who require their services on a regular basis, so that much of their business is like the contract business of the larger firms. The independents also tend to make greater use of the public taxicab stands near shopping centres.

As in Sarnia, most of the taxicabs (including those not owned by the firms) are double shifted. This is clearly a simultaneous relationship between high fixed costs and double shifting, whether the high fixed costs be licence rentals (as in Toronto) or high concession fees (as in Sarnia and Windsor). The high concession fees provide an incentive for owners to double shift their taxicabs, and the prevalence of double shifting enables the firms to charge high concession fees. Since the marginal costs of operating a dispatching service and providing contracts cannot be much greater in these cities (particularly in Windsor, where average and marginal costs may be quite similar) than in London or Toronto, one imagines that the present firms are earning some economic profits. Entry has, to some extent, affected who receives these economic profits, but the profits themselves are not likely to disappear, because of the economies of scale which exist.

6 Kitchener / Waterloo

Entry is regulated into the taxicab industries throughout the entire Regional Municipality of Waterloo by the regional government. This study examines conditions only in the twin cities of Kitchener and Waterloo. Entry is restricted to maintain a ratio of approximately one taxicab per 1300 residents. A further restriction is that taxicabs from one city may operate between the two cities but not within the other city. Fares for the two cities are set; there appears to be no allowance for hourly group fares in the bylaws.

All three companies in the two cities are co-operatives with similar sets of bylaws and with an owner-driver acting as co-op manager. Unlike the firms studied elsewhere, in Kitchener / Waterloo the co-ops schedule the drivers and second drivers according to historical demand patterns. Their feeling is that this scheduling reduces their time between trips and reduces their number of empty miles, but this belief could not be tested. The schedules are rotated so that all owners, during a year, have equal proportions of high demand and low demand periods for their operations. Second drivers are generally paid a 40 per cent commission in Kitchener / Waterloo. There is a stated policy of the co-ops to keep the membership diverse via single-owner-drivers to prohibit one person from gaining dominance in a firm. Most of the cabs are double shifted, but the second shifts are scheduled by the co-ops, and so there is not the split between double-shifted and single-shifted taxicabs that exists elsewhere.

Perhaps the most interesting feature of the Kitchener / Waterloo taxicab industry is that while the licences are scarce and command a value, most (if not all) of the licence value is appropriated by the co-ops through large initiation fees. Someone wishing to join Waterloo Cab must pay the co-op $8500; in Kitchener the initiation fee is between $10,000 and $11,000. The co-ops then divide these proceeds among their members. The co-ops have pre-empted the regional licensing commission by making co-op membership (rather than licence ownership) the scarce and valuable commodity. Membership in the co-op allows the member to earn some rents on his licence and to receive additional rents whenever a new owner is admitted to membership. Because memberships cannot be transferred privately, those leaving a co-op can receive little or no capital gain on the sale of their licences. Consequently, there are fairly high barriers to exit from the industry in addition to the barriers to entry. The barriers to entry are created by the regulatory regime in conjunction with the economies of scale in dispatching and contract negotiation; the barriers to exit are created by the inability to sell one's co-op membership privately.

People are willing to pay the higher initiation fees for two reasons. The first is that entry into the industry is restricted, generating the potential for earning rents. The second is that a person, once a co-op member, can receive a portion of these rents as his share of the initiation fees paid by others joining the co-op. There is a waiting list of non-owner drivers affiliated with each of the co-ops wishing to become members of the co-ops. New members are admitted as licences become available on the basis of committee judgment which considers seniority on the waiting list as well as work experience and personal characteristics.

7 Los Angeles

Taxicab regulation in the Los Angeles area provides a considerable contrast to that in the other municipalities studied. With two important exceptions, firms are granted franchises to operate in specific geographic areas. The franchises are usually, but not always, single-firm monopoly franchises, giving the firm sole operating authority for its area. The taxicabs themselves are also licensed, but generally (though not always) the firms are free to add taxicabs to their fleet as the demand increases.

Generally speaking, the metropolitan area of Los Angeles has extremely low population density, a well-developed freeway system, and sufficiently high incomes that people there rely on private auto transportation to a much greater extent than do people in, say, Toronto or Washington. One explanation offered for this population dispersion is that until the early 1960s, building codes discouraged the construction of tall buildings because of the fear of earthquakes. Because of the population dispersion, average trip lengths are higher, fares are higher, and waiting time between trips is greater. Also, the taxicab / population ratios are very low, one per 5000 residents or even more in some areas. The cruising business is minimal in the Los Angeles area, but a sizeable amount of the business does come from stands at the airports, major hotels, and recreation centres. This study examines the industry only within the City of Los Angeles proper.

From the early 1940s until 1976, Los Angeles was virtually monopolized by

Yellow Cabs, which, with a few brief periods of exception, had an exclusive franchise. In 1976 Yellow failed to meet several of its workmen's compensation premium payments, and in December 1976 the firm declared bankruptcy. During the ensuing few months municipal politicians and regulators worked feverishly to try to decide what changes should be made in their control of the industry. In the meantime, many former drivers with Yellow started driving their own cars as taxicabs. City authorities had mixed feelings about these independent, unregulated taxicabs: they were pleased to have taxicab service being provided to the city, yet they feared chaos resulting from having the industry unregulated. As new regulations were devised and as new franchises were being considered, the decision-makers decided that there were two important goals for their policies. One was to make room in the industry for the independent taxicab owner-drivers, partly to reward them for providing service for the city after Yellow went bankrupt and partly due to general pressure to allow and even encourage small business to thrive. The second goal was to reduce the city's dependence on a single firm, and so several franchises were considered for most areas of the city. The independents were required, however, to join one of two approved associations of independent taxicab owners.

All taxicabs were allowed to provide service to or from the Los Angeles International Airport. The airport had six stands able to contain six cabs each and a holding area for seventy more. Taxicab traffic at the airport is often heavy, giving rise to congestion and allegations of unscrupulous behaviour on the part of some drivers. To help control the situation, the airport has its own taxicab management personnel to direct taxicab traffic and impose fines on drivers not obeying their regulations.

Another concern of the city authorities is that too many of the drivers will want to provide service to the lucrative stands and to the airport, so that service to customers in residential areas will be inadequate. This fear, clearly, is based on ignorance of the substitution principle in economics, that if too many drivers seek fares at the stands and at the airport the waiting time between fares will increase and equate the expected marginal profitability of providing all types of service. But rather than use market forces to allocate taxicab services, the city has made the provision of adequate service to all parts of an area a condition of the franchises, with fines imposed for failure to provide adequate service. Adequate service is expected to result in part because most franchises specify that the firm maintain a *minimum* number of taxicabs in service. In addition, however, the city requires that the firms answer telephone calls within forty-five seconds, and that taxicabs pick up their customers within fifteen minutes of the time the call is made. The city employs people to place numerous test calls for each firm in each service area and pays a driver responding to a test call three dollars.

Usually franchises are required to pay 1 per cent of their gross receipts to the city for the franchise. In addition, penalties for inadequate service response are levied.

To avoid having a single firm emerge as a monopolist again, Los Angeles not only issues multiple franchises for most service areas but also imposes maximum numbers of taxicab permits on each of the three large firms. The revived Yellow Cab Co. has a maximum of 302 permits, and each of the independent associations is limited to 176 members. Most of the independents fear that if these maxima were not imposed, Yellow would expand very rapidly and drive them all out of business.

It is peculiar that in Los Angeles though many firms have the option of expanding the size of their fleets people are still waiting to pay current members of the independent associations $12,000 for their membership slots. Why should anyone pay so much to earn monopoly rents as an independent owner-driver when the other firms can expand and compete away these rents? Certainly some of the other firms are indeed expanding. The high membership price may reflect in part the incomplete adjustments which have taken place in Los Angeles after the bankruptcy of Yellow. It is also possible, however, that many of the drivers would prefer to work without workmen's compensation and unemployment insurance coverage and want to be able to hide some of their earnings from the Internal Revenue Service. These drivers may be quite willing to pay such initial sums; that behaviour would explain how franchised firms with minimum size constraints can co-exist with independents having maximum size constraints and whose memberships command a high price. The independents, presumably, are willing to pay even more because they expect to receive income tax benefits as owner-drivers and because of the non-pecuniary benefits they perceive accruing to themselves. In other words, drivers wishing no workmen's compensation or unemployment insurance might be willing to pay $1000 a year to avoid paying for this insurance; they are willing to pay the equivalent of $1600 a year to be independent owner-drivers because they also expect to pay less income tax and because of additional non-pecuniary sources of utility. In fact, however, most drivers probably would like to purchase as much as is required for employees by state legislation. Those who do not want the state-enacted insurance and who put a low value on the non-pecuniary aspects of independent ownership probably drive for the major companies; others, depending on the strengths of their preferences, prefer to belong to, and drive for, the independent associations.

Conclusion
It is apparent from the case studies that the taxicab industry has not evolved in a uniform manner in all cities. Clearly, the dispatch and radio business assumes much more importance in some centres, predominantly the smaller ones. As a

result, there may be room for only a couple of taxicab firms in these cities. In other, primarily larger centres, dispatching plays a lesser role as cruising produces more business.

Virtually all cities regulate taxi fares to some degree. Fare regulation has some merit in protecting consumers who might otherwise face an unequal bargaining position. Even if the bargaining strengths are equal, fare regulation can still perform a useful function as an information dispensing tool.

Regardless of the size of the city and the structure of its taxi industry, it is clear that there is no need for entry controls on taxicabs. The usual rationales for entry regulation – (1) reducing negative externalities such as congestion or noise; (2) maintaining consumer protection; (3) ensuring an adequate income stream for industry members; and (4) ensuring a stable provision of services – do not appear to justify restrictions on access to the taxicab industry. Without entry controls, there is considerable capacity flexibility which enables the industry to adapt quickly to changes in demand.

Ontario Economic Council Research Studies